RUGBY

A Guide for Players, Coaches, and Spectators

RUGBY

A Guide for Players, Coaches, and Spectators

A. JON PRUSMACK

HAWTHORN BOOKS, INC.
Publishers/NEW YORK
A Howard & Wyndham Company

RUGBY: A GUIDE FOR PLAYERS, COACHES, AND SPECTATORS

Copyright © 1979 by A. Jon Prusmack. Copyright under International and Pan-American Copyright Conventions. All rights reserved, including the right to reproduce this book or portions thereof in any form, except for the inclusion of brief quotations in a review. All inquiries should be addressed to Hawthorn Books, Inc., 260 Madison Avenue, New York, New York 10016. This book was manufactured in the United States of America and published simultaneously in Canada by Prentice-Hall of Canada, Limited, 1870 Birchmount Road, Scarborough, Ontario.

Library of Congress Catalog Card Number: 78-65404.
ISBN: 0-8015-6490-5
1 2 3 4 5 6 7 8 9 10

CONTENTS

FOREWORD

Rugby, while played in the United States since the late nineteenth century has, nevertheless, been totally overshadowed by gridiron football and, in recent years, by soccer. It is interesting to note that both of these games evolved from the framework of rugby.

Rugby is essentially being rediscovered in the United States. Many U.S. players and coaches envision the game as a football collision match, when in reality rugby is a fluid contact sport that is much more akin to hockey, lacrosse, and even basketball.

Most of the literature of the sport has been authored by highly respected and renowned individuals overseas who have grown up with the game since the diaper stage. And in this context they assume a certain level of understanding and proficiency from rugby players. In most cases, Americans don't have this—because no tradition of the game has yet to establish itself, as in baseball, football, and basketball. If Woody Hayes wrote about gridiron football he would assume a certain degree of understanding among his readers. Such is the case with the rugby books originating in other countries.

This book is meant to serve as a guide for players, coaches, and spectators. Its objectives are simple: to provide a historical perspective of rugby, and to explain and relate the fundamentals of the game to Americans.

Americans have skills developed from their games which, rather than being discarded or ignored, can be applied to rugby. This book also tries to integrate what we can do with what we have, instead of learning all new tricks.

ACKNOWLEDGMENTS

I wish to thank the Rugby Football Union in England, the United States of America Rugby Football Union, especially Ray Cornbill, coach of the United States National team, and *Rugby* magazine for their cooperation. I would also like to thank my wife, Patrice, who not only put up with my rugby fanaticism for ten years but also became involved with the game as a photojournalist. Her action photography captures the spirit of rugby and gives life to the text.

1

IN THE BEGINNING

Rugby football has a history that can be traced back thousands of years to the first recorded foot-the-ball games. Chronicles have been written as far back as the Han Dynasty in China, where men played a kick-the-ball type of game to celebrate the emperor's birthday. In ancient Greece a kind of foot-the-ball game was also played, in which free use of the hands was part of the action. And the Romans, adapting the game from the Greeks, played a running, handling, kicking game called harpustum. This name was derived from the Greek verb "to seize," and the game may well have been the forerunner of what we call rugby football.

Harpustum was a war game. The Roman army used it both to entertain and condition troops. It was played on a rectangle of land very similar to a rugby pitch, and there were similar in-goal areas as well as crude goal posts. Play was begun when the two sides were lined up at midfield facing each other. The total number of players was not fixed, but each side needed an equal number. A roundish ball was then thrown between the two phalanxes of men. The objective was quite simple—to move the ball across the other side's goal line by any means—running, kicking, and handling the ball. Very little is written regarding the specifics, such as infractions and penalties, but the referee was a Roman officer who always carried a short sword.

As the Roman Empire expanded, harpustum found its way to the British Isles. Conscripting Britons into the Roman army introduced the game to the local population, and it became quite popular. Historians have even referred to the British holiday of Shrove Tuesday as the commemoration of a football match at Derby in 217 A.D., when a local side beat the Roman army garrison.

As the Romans left Britain the game of football became assimilated into local custom, with nearby towns playing each other. Many times it was the focal point of local celebrations and festivals. And by the twelfth century a form of foot-the-ball was an accepted part of society wherein each town or village cheered its side to victory as it also tended to its wounded.

It was during the next several hundred years that foot-the-ball games degenerated into a state of near warfare. Rivalries took on the semblance of crusades: Even killing one's opposite number was not unheard of. The situation became so bad that Edward II and James I outlawed the playing of any form of foot-the-ball. Anyone caught playing the game was severely fined. By the end of the sixteenth century and early part of the seventeenth century a crude form of village football had regained a modicum of respectability, and some general rules were created that prevented the game from turning into a local holocaust.

Throughout Great Britain Shrove Tuesday was celebrated with a foot-the-ball match. Even Oliver Cromwell, a footballer in his own right, supported the playing of football games during his Commonwealth period. The character of this early game of foot-the-ball was a vicious concoction of what we call soccer and a very crude form of rugby. The objective was basically the same— take the ball across the opposition's goal area and put it between the two goal posts. The ball (a pig's bladder surrounded by leather) was kicked—while everyone "hacked," or kicked, each other's shins—or carried into the in-goal area. When a goal was scored, the scoring side received one point and then the teams switched goals.

The advent of the Industrial Revolution in England in the eighteenth century caused more and more people to work in factories. The result was less and less free time for leisure. On holidays few people wanted to play football—or for that matter, even watch football. Only in small rural towns did the game of foot-the-ball have any support.

It was not until the mid-nineteenth century, when the Factory Acts were passed in England, that some leisure time became available to the working person. The initial reintroduction of the foot-the-ball games came not from the working class, nor from the countryside villages and towns, however, but from the new schools that were forming in England—the public, or as we call them, private schools. These schools were designed as training grounds for England's future leaders. And since students did not have time to indulge in the individual activities of the past aristocracy, that is, hunting, shooting, riding, and fishing, acceptance of the old village games became part of their corporate education. Such a school was Rugby School.

1

Rugby at Rugby School (ca. 1830)

2a

The Eton Wall game owes its origin and development entirely to local circumstances. Basically, eleven players from each side tried to move a ball along the wall toward a goal area at each end of the wall. Players used padding and supposedly the wall was padded.

2b

An early scrummage in the Winchester School game. This football game was similar to the Rugby School Game though scrummaging was more of a "flying wedge" than a method to start play. In addition, the field was enclosed by a fence.

Each public school played its own form of foot-the-ball. Rules were based on the traditions of the old village festival games. But each school modified the game in order to fit its particular grounds. For example, schools that had constricted playing areas used fewer players, less kicking, and a smaller ball, and they practiced much in-tight massing of players, known as scrummaging. The most famous of these games was the Eton Wall Game. The game was played on a pitch 120 yards long with about a 10-foot-high wall on the one side running the entire length of the pitch, and a touch line 6 yards parallel to it. Action was basically one long continuous scrum. At Rugby School, however, which had a spacious playing area called the Close, the game was more open, had more players, utilized downfield kicking, was played with a larger ball, and had a bit of running and handling to it.

By the mid-nineteenth century two versions of the game began to develop: a dribbling versus a handling game. Rules began to be written down and "laws" began to take shape. It is interesting to point out, however, that these early rules were rough and were drawn up, *not* by an adult rules committee, but by students of

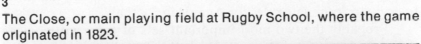

3

The Close, or main playing field at Rugby School, where the game originated in 1823.

high school age who wanted the games to be more than just undisciplined schoolboy riots. Similarly, it took a young American college student, Walter Camp, more than one hundred years later, to begin to formulate rules for American football.

Probably the two most important sets of rules written were those of Harrow and Rugby School. By 1830 the schoolboys had so codified the game at Harrow that it really was a book of laws. Under no circumstances could anyone run with the ball. The only exception was when a ball was caught on the fly. Then the catcher could run three paces in any direction and then kick it. After the kick everyone rushed forward.

The Game at Rugby

William Webb Ellis. . . . He was an admirable cricketer, but was generally regarded as inclined to take unfair advantages in football.[1]

[1] Written by Matthew Holbeche Bloxam in The Rugby School *Meteor*, December 22, 1880, as published by *Centenary History of the Rugby Football Union*, by U. S. Titley and Ross McWhirter (Redwood Press Ltd.: Thowbridge & London, 1970).

3a
Two sides before a match at Rugby School, ca. 1880. Note that everyone out on the field played. The dimensions were 130 yards by 80 yards. It is interesting to observe their outfits, very similar to the early United States football togs with their longish pants (knicker-type), jerseys, and small caps. As the game progressed in England, pants became shorts. As the game evolved into football in the United States, the pants became lined with padding.

At Rugby School though, no such rigid code existed; custom held that any player catching the ball could kick it back toward the opposition. He could run backwards with the ball to get some momentum for the kick forward, but advancing the ball forward on the run was banned. An old Rugbeian, Matthew Holbeche Bloxam, painted a picture of what the game of foot-the-ball was like at the time of William Webb Ellis, ca. 1823:

> When all had assembled in the Close, two of the best players in the school commenced choosing in, one for each side. After choosing in about a score [20] on each side, a somewhat rude division of the remaining fags [boys within the English public schools who do menial services for other boys of a higher grade], half of whom were sent to keep goal on the one side, the other half to the opposite goal for the same purpose.

Any fag, though not chosen in, might follow up on that side to the goal of which he was attached.

Some of these were ready enough to mingle in the fray; others judiciously kept half-back, watching their opportunity for a casual kick, which was not infrequently awarded them. Few and simple were the rules of the game: touch on the sides of the ground was marked out and no one was allowed to run with the ball in his grasp toward the opposite goal. It was football and not handball, plenty of hacking [kicking at the shins] but little struggling.[2]

Bloxam, though not an eyewitness to Ellis' action, was a law student at Rugby and it was on his testimony that many years later the full credit was finally given to Ellis for his deed at Rugby School. Bloxam wrote:

In the latter half of 1823, some fifty-seven years ago, originated, though without any premeditation, that change in one of the rules which more than any other has since distinguished the Rugby School game from the Association rules.

A boy of the name Ellis—William Webb Ellis—a town boy and a foundationer, who at the age of nine entered the school after the mid-summer holidays in 1816, who in the second half-year of 1823, was, I believe, a praeposter [a senior student], whilst playing Bigside at football in that half-year, caught the ball in his arms. This being so, according to the then rules, he ought to have retired back as far as he pleased, without parting with the ball, for the combatants on the opposite side could only advance to the spot where he caught the ball and were unable to rush forward until he had either punted it or placed it for someone else to kick, for it was by means of these placed kicks that most of the goals were in those days kicked, but the moment it touched the ground the opposite side might rush on. Ellis, for the first time, disregarded this rule, and on catching the ball, instead of retiring backwards, rushed forward with the ball in his hands

[2]Ibid., p. 29.

toward the opposite goal, with what result as to the game I know not, neither do I know how this infringement of a well-known rule was followed up, or when it became, as it is now, the standing rule.[3]

What Ellis did was tagged by his classmates as "running in" the ball. And, according to most gentlemen at the school, his action was akin to the ancient village foot-the-ball tactic of trying to force the ball downfield and into the goal area by compact masses of charging bodies kicking and running with it.

By 1841, the boys at Rugby School had decided that "running in" the ball was their game and it was codified into their set of rules. Running with the ball was legal as long as the run was made after catching the ball on the fly—no bounces allowed. It wasn't until 1874 that the rules were amended to allow a player to pick up a loose ball and run with it.

Obviously, with two conflicting views on how to play the same game, a split was inevitable. In 1863 the rugby rules men, led by the Blackheath Club, walked out of a meeting of the Football Association. The remaining body thus formulated the rules for association football, or as we call it, soccer, and the other group formed their rugby association—not to be confused with the Rugby Football Union, which came into existence in January 1871.

By the late 1860s the Football Association began to differentiate its dribbling from the handling game. For one, the free kick at goal after making a fair catch or mark was abolished. The crossbar was replaced by a tape and only kick shots below the tape counted. The *coup de grace* occurred in 1870 when the Football Association banned forever any player handling the ball—save one, the goalkeeper. Football was to be foot-the-ball, i.e., soccer, using the feet, not phalanxes of players, i.e., rugby, heaving and shoving up and down the field.

The basic reason why the rugby and association men split was the hacking, or kicking indiscriminately, at the ball and therefore your opponent's shins. The rugby people, quite surprisingly, felt it was a test of manhood and courage and should remain. The

[3]Ibid., p. 31

association people thought it just made a hopeless confusion of the game. A few years later the rugby association also dropped the hacking rule. By now, the only way to win at rugby was through hard, almost blind, shoving. Early matches were twenty to a side with fifteen forwards. The forwards' principal job was to keep the ball in tight scrummage formation and either dribble it downfield or nestle it within their mass and march down the field.

The backline, or backfield, was composed of two goalkeepers who were "full-back" from the pack of forwards; another who was "three-quarters" back between the goal area and the pack; and two men who were "half-back." It was these half-backs and the three-quarters who waited for the ball to slip or pop out of the mass. But instead of opening up the game by racing downfield, the backs normally took the ball and piled back into the forwards. Open field action was at a minimum.

While both rugby men and association men were from the same background—public school, university, and club football—each side viewed the game differently. The rugby camaraderie, while accepted everywhere, was most enjoyed by the wealthier rugby clubs in the south of England. It was the camaraderie that provided their reason for playing. Rugby football was for fun only. In the north of England a different attitude developed. The fierce loyalties of the northern and midland cities and towns, and the few moments of glory the game provided for the working-class player, could not be fathomed by those in the south. The association people recognized this conflict and provided for growth that eventually reconciled amateur and professional status. The Rugby Union did not. The result was another split or schism in the football ranks.

The Great Divide

Association football saw the game developing with more and more spectators demanding better and better performances from their teams. Players would need more time to practice in order to produce, and this would take away from working time and therefore reduce their wages. Association football endorsed payments to its players alongside the growth of the amateur game.

The Rugby Union administrators did not see their game in such a light. Players on northern clubs wanted compensation for time off or broken-time payments for training and traveling. The Rugby Union forbade the clubs to exercise such payments. In 1895 twenty northern clubs resigned from the Union and formed their own northern union, later re-formed and called the Rugby League. The rift that split the Union was less than one dollar per player in broken-time payments. Today, Rugby League is played both as an amateur sport and as a professional sport. Rugby Union is an amateur game only.

The differences between Rugby Union and Rugby League are not that acute. The one novel idea that the League introduced was the concept of set possession. And this has carried itself into our American football. In Union rules a tackled player must release the ball so that the continuous free flow of action is maintained. In League, the tackled player's team is allowed to keep possession for five plays and if there is no score, a set scrum develops.

Rugby Football Comes to America

While rugby football originated in the villages of England, no such football evolution occurred in the United States. Foot-the-ball was introduced in the colleges for the American rich. The cities and towns in nineteenth-century America were just too spread out for any meaningful team sporting activities to prosper.

The form of foot-the-ball played in the States, needless to say, was a mixture of rugby and soccer. Handling the ball was just a means of stopping it, not advancing it. The first intercollegiate football game in 1869 between Rutgers and Princeton was more of a soccer match than any football game as we envision it today. They used a round ball and the objective was to kick the ball through the opposition's goal. No running was permitted. Rutgers won 6 goals to 4 goals.

In 1870 Columbia University joined this intercollegiate group, followed by Yale in 1872. A year later these four schools agreed on the rules for a dribbling game along the lines of association football. Simultaneously, at Harvard the students were playing the "Boston game," which was basically English rugby. Part of this was due to a home-and-away series with McGill University of Montreal, Canada, which was popular since everyone enjoyed going to Canada to play.

.It was also about this time that one of the first international rugby touring teams visited the United States. Eton College, visiting Yale, introduced a handling game with only eleven players. The match was so much more enjoyable than the twenty-to-a-side that Yale pressured the intercollegiate association to adopt the eleven-man rule. It was a few more years, however, before that adoption took effect. In 1876 the intercollegiate association scrapped the dribbling game for the more exciting handling game and the Rugby Union rules. But it took a seventeen-year-old halfback from Yale, Walter Camp, to change the course of football in the United States from rugby to what is now known as gridiron football.

It is interesting to note that without Walter Camp and his two fundamental rule changes, Rugby Union might have been *the* game in the United States today instead of gridiron. Camp's first dramatic change was to get the rules committee to agree to reduce the number of players from fifteen to eleven. His second most critical change dealt with possession. The set scrum was the standard method of initiating play and determining who was to get possession after an infraction. When one side put the ball in, it was fairly sure of possession, but never guaranteed it. Camp argued that the side putting the ball in should be guaranteed possession so that appropriate and planned attacking and defending action could be taken. By adopting this rule, the basis for play calling and the whole ritual of huddles was established. While Rugby League had a possession rule, still applicable today, it was based on the contention that after the ball is won from the scrum, the team winning it has five downs with the ball to score. If the team doesn't score, then there is a set scrum and the winner of the scrum has the five downs. It's very fast.

The scrimmage line would now take place when the hooker (in the center of the scrum) put the ball in play by "snapping," instead of "heeling," it back with his foot. Instead of a scrumhalf (because the scrum was evolving into a line of forwards versus a pack of forwards), the man receiving the ball was labeled a *quarterback*. This was because he was between the halfbacks and

3b

The early stages of gridiron after the guaranteed possession rule was established (ca. 1885). Note that with the new rule, the hooker "snapped" the ball back and the props aligned to "block" rather than "bind." This resulted in the open scrummage. The early uniforms were essentially the same as worn for rugby. As blocking increased, helmets and shoulder pads became part of the equipment.

---

the forwards, and thus a quarter of the distance. Even with these changes, field action was much akin to rugby: lateral passes out to the backline; tackling around the waist; kicking for touch; rucks and mauls; and an innovation called the "flying wedge." But the die was cast. And with these initial changes gridiron began to assume its own style of play. By 1888 blocking and tackling below the waist had been legalized. By 1900 the only vestige of rugby in American gridiron football was the line-out—and it was soon abolished. Gridiron football had degenerated into a violent and dangerous shambles of a game. In fact, President Theodore Roosevelt threatened college administrators that if they did not "clean up" the game he would ban it. The result was the introduction of the forward pass in 1906 as a means of opening up the game and neutralizing the violence. This almost retired rugby.

4
The 1920 Olympic side

How Rugby Survived

Early collegiate football consisted primarily of rugby matches. Many colleges and universities did not adopt Camp's suggestions and subsequent rule changes. For example, in 1905, Camp's version of football was so destructive in terms of physical abuse that the University of California at Berkeley, Stanford University, Santa Clara, St. Mary's, and the University of Nevada at Reno dropped Camp's game. English rugby was revived and was played throughout the country until the end of World War I. In fact, rugby was so popular on the West Coast that foreign touring sides stopped by for a match or two. In 1913 an official All Black side (the name of the team) from New Zealand played an unofficial All-American side. The Americans lost 51–3. On the East Coast, the Ivy League schools maintained rugby football as an exclusive "club" sport versus a varsity sport, a condition that still exists today.

In 1920 and 1924, rugby was still being played in the Olympics. And the Americans wanted to compete. The 1920 U.S. Olympic committee felt that since California was the only state playing rugby, the state should finance its players' fares to Europe. The Olympic committee overlooked the fact that one of the warmup matches for the U.S. Olympic side was against a Metropolitan New York XV in Newark. The Olympians won 21–3.

In the finale at Antwerp Stadium before 55,000 spectators, the Americans defeated the French 8–0. The French were so upset at the defeat that they invited the Americans to stay awhile, tour the country, and play a few matches. The United States team won all the tour matches, with victories over Lyons 26–3, South of France representative side 11–3, and a Southwestern France representative side 6–3. By the time of the final match against France a month later most of the Americans had gone home, so a somewhat less proficient side gave the French a scrappy game before losing 14–5.

In 1924 the U.S. Olympic committee again would not allocate funds for rugby. The U.S. Olympic committee did not want to be embarrassed by a disastrous defeat, so the Californians once again were forced to dig into their own pockets. The U.S. team won a second gold medal in rugby when they defeated France 17–3 in front of 50,000 fans at Colombes Stadium. Except for the glory of the two Olympic victories, rugby began to disappear from the sports scene during the twenties, but before it died out completely, three territorial unions developed: the Eastern Rugby Union, the Midwest Rugby Union, and the Pacific Rugby Union.

5
The 1924 United States Olympic side

The Eastern Rugby Union

In the twenties, rugby clubs really did not have any formal status or association. Since gridiron had replaced rugby as the major contact sport in colleges, rugby became a club or intramural affair. The first club outside of the colleges was the New York Rugby Club, which was formed in 1929. It was followed in 1930 by the Harvard Rugby Club and the Yale Rugby Club. Princeton formed a team in 1931, and this group was joined by the Long Island RFC, the French RFC, The Pilgrims RFC, Lafayette College RFC, St. John's University RFC, and Hofstra College RFC during the next two years.

In the East, rugby was a spring game. Interclub matches were arranged via tournaments, so the need for a coordinating body was not so necessary. But in 1934 Cambridge University toured the East, and in order to coordinate the matches as well as put together an All-Star side, a degree of organization was necessary. Thus the Eastern Rugby Union was born, with a litter of ten clubs. By 1943 the ERU had grown to twelve clubs. During the

6
The New York Rugby team defeating the Harvard fifteen in the opening game of the season at the Polo Grounds, New York City, April 2, 1934.

war and postwar years the ERU was inoperative. In 1954 the ERU formally reactivated itself with seven clubs. It was during this time also that the colleges rapidly rediscovered the game and adopted it as a club sport versus a varsity sport. That is nearly the status of it today. Very few colleges and universities offer the game as a varsity sport. It is treated as a club activity, much like the glee club. The rationale is that the game is for players, not coaches. Even the service academies keep it a club activity.

By 1961 there were 28 member clubs in the ERU. In that year also the ERU sent its first official representative side to play against Quebec Province. The ERU lost 6–3. By 1967 the ERU had grown to 44 clubs with subunions starting to spring up. And in the next ten years the ERU grew over 600 percent, overseeing more than 275 clubs in 12 subunions, 17 clubs in areas where there were no local unions, 7 referee societies, and 20 women's clubs, all covering an area from Florida to Maine. Probably one of the biggest thrills for the ERU was in 1976 when an All-Star side almost upset France, losing 16–12 in the French Bicentennial Tour of the U.S.

The Midwest Rugby Union

The birth of the Midwest Union was spearheaded by the formation of the Chicago Rugby Club (not to be confused with the Chicago Lions) in 1932. The club was so strong that in 1938 it topped a Canadian representative side from Manitoba 13–3. But like the East and West Coasts, there was still no formal organization to administer the burgeoning clubs. It took a quarter of a century for ten clubs to meet and formalize the Midwest Rugby Union in 1964. By 1976 the Midwest Union had more than 300 clubs in 7 subunions.

The Pacific Coast

Rugby was *the* game on the West Coast in the early part of the twentieth century. Gridiron was for, well, cavemen, and the better schools looked at it as a resurgence of cromagnon activity. But as the rules for gridiron changed, so did the acceptance of the game. The Olympic victories in 1920 and 1924, while sisyphean tasks by anyone's criteria, could not stem the tide of gridiron popularity.

In the thirties both the Northern California Union and the Southern California Union were formed. Each union numbered around 40 clubs. And this remained fairly steady until the 1950s. During this period and into the sixties, the game exploded in California. To accommodate this growth the Pacific Coast Union was formed, combining the two California unions. Today this union includes the new northwest subunion and covers the entire West Coast from Mexico to Canada, totalling almost 150 clubs.

The Western Rugby Union

Geographically, the Western Rugby Union is the largest. It covers over one million square miles. It is also the youngest and emerged as a result of two natural dividers—the Rockies in the West and the Mississippi River in the East. Rugby started in the

West in the major cities, such as Kansas City and Denver. Soon more and more clubs were formed, giving rise to five local or subunions: The Beehive, The Eastern Rockies, The Heart of America, The Missouri, and The Texas. In March 1975 these five unions joined and formed the umbrella territorial union, the Western Rugby Union. With four territorial unions now formed, the stage was set for the next logical step—the formation of the United States of America Rugby Football Union.

The Formation of the United States Rugby Union

Officially the union was established in Chicago on June 7, 1975. Representatives of the four territorial unions met in a generally cooperative atmosphere. The need for a recognized United States administrative body was obvious to all who had involved themselves in the game over the past years. How else would an official U.S. national side play internationals against England, France, or the rest of the rugby nations? The rugby playing nations take formality very seriously and nothing less than an official United States Union would suffice in arranging future internationals.

The first attempt at organizing a union, though, was in 1968. Coincidentally, it was also in Chicago, and many of the same players in 1968 were also in the lineup in 1975. The primary reason

7
Founders of the United States of America Rugby Football Union, Chicago, 1975

8

The first United States national side to play Canada in Vancouver, May 21, 1977. The United States lost the match.

9

The first United States national side to play England at Twickenham, Hampshire, England. The United States was defeated.

10
The United States on the attack with its first international victory,
a 12–7 win over Canada, May 1978

the union made it in 1975 rather than in 1968 was a result of a positive attitude coupled by a realistic appraisal that it had to be done. The game was growing too rapidly in the States and some sort of national control and organization was imperative.

Since the formation of the United States Union, the national body has organized internationals with Australia (January 1976, United States 12, Australia 24); France (June 1976, U.S. 14, France 33); set up a home-and-away series with the Canadians (Canada won the first match 17–6, while the U.S. won the second 12–7); toured England with a finale against an England XV at the mecca of rugby, Twickenham. Unfortunately, the United States also lost 37–12, but it was a start.

No matter which way the game goes internationally, the essence of good rugby is good play. And good play starts with a thorough and solid understanding of the fundamentals of the game—its objectives, its principles, its basics, and its strategy. The core of this book is devoted to these important aspects of rugby football.

2
THE BASICS

What's It All About?

According to the laws, the object of the game is that two teams of fifteen players each, observing fair play and with a sporting spirit should, by carrying, passing, and kicking the ball, score as many points as possible. The team scoring the greatest number of points is the winner of the match.

While this is the legal description of rugby, it leaves most people grasping for more detail. For two forty-minute halves with just a five-minute break, thirty players bang heads and whip an oversized-looking football around on a pitch (field) 100 meters long by 69 meters wide with no time-outs and with no substitution.*

The players attempt to advance the ball over the try line (goal line) by running with it, kicking it, or by passing it laterally or backwards—never forward. Only the ball carrier is allowed to be tackled. There is no blocking. There are no shoulder pads or helmets. And there will be no halftime show (see fig. 1).

---

*According to the laws, any delay in game must be made up at the end of the half in which it occurred. Also, only injured players may be replaced and no more than two per match. Refer to laws 3 and 5 in chapter 8.

Besides being a running, handling, kicking, and tackling game, rugby football is also a thinking game because players must understand what they are going to do, where they are going to do it, and when they should do it—all in a second. It's not enough just to know basic skills. A player must know how and exactly when to apply these skills repeatedly in game situations. Just knowing how to pass or how to kick in practice is not enough—a player must understand the whole scheme of what is supposed to go on out on the field and how he or she should perform. And probably more so than in any other game, the player must be aware of him- or herself as part of the whole flow of action. To play rugby without understanding what basic guidelines govern action on the field of play is like driving a car blindfolded—you know if you turn on the engine and step on the gas the car will go, but you don't know where.

A solid foundation of the basic individual and group skills nailed together with an understanding of what principles a team should follow as a unit is very important to playing and making the game more enjoyable. In addition, attitude and approach to rugby is important. Sports such as basketball, lacrosse and soccer are closer to rugby in attitude and action than football. Football is basically a static game—a little running, a lot of huddling. The other sports mentioned all exhibit constant ball movement linked by fluid and continuous player action. Rugby play is designed to score points via movement rather than force. This is not to say that football players are not good rugby players or they will not be good rugby players. On the contrary, many Americans who first got into the game started out after their college gridiron careers were over. So the bulk of Americans now playing rugby are ex-footballers. The commentary is only on how to approach playing the game mentally, not who should play.

Many Americans, though, do approach playing rugby with a misguided football doctrine—the "hit 'em" syndrome. Yes, rugby is a contact game. Football, though, is a collision game. There's a big difference. The ball in rugby moves as a function of bodies trying to avoid each other. In football, the ball moves as a function of bodies colliding.

The essence of rugby is this constant ball movement. Remember, a moving ball can always travel faster than a running player.

And a ball held too long or tied up is not a moving ball. Rugby is not "three yards and a cloud of dust." Rugby is movement—a fluid game with strategy and tactics dictated by team personnel and constantly changing field position. To accomplish all this effectively, players must understand what principles should guide them on the field-of-play.

In rugby, linemen are called "forwards." They consist of eight players and are called "the pack." The backfield, properly called the backline, holds the remaining seven. But all fifteen players can run with the ball at any time.

Play can be started in two ways after the ball has been blown dead by the single referee—the set scrum and the line-out. The scrum is used when action *on* the field-of-play has stopped and must be started again. A line-out is used to begin play when action has stopped because the ball went *out* of the field-of-play but between the two goal lines.

A kick-off starts a game and is also made *after* a score (called a try and worth four points). The team that scored receives the kick-off. The drop-out is used to begin play again after the ball has gone beyond the goal line and is downed by the defending side, or after it has sailed out of bounds via the in-goal area. For details consult the laws that are included at the back of this book.

Finally, there are the ruck and the maul. These describe action *with* the ball on the field-of-play. A ruck occurs when the ball is loose on the ground and players from both sides try to gain possession of it by using their feet. A maul, on the other hand, occurs when a player with the ball is stopped, but not tackled, and cannot advance forward. In this situation, hands are used.

The Four Principles of Play

These four principles are not original but have developed out of British analytical studies done on the game. In trying to determine what essential elements link together forming overall team play, four principles emerged: Go Forward, Support, Keep the Ball Alive, and Pressure the Opposition.

Go Forward. If you are not moving toward the opposition's goal line, then you're not going forward. It's that simple. Scoring

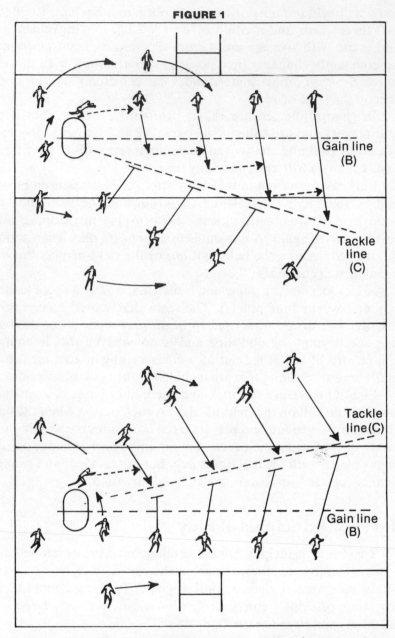

FIGURE 1

Gain line
(B)

Tackle
line
(C)

Tackle
line (C)

Gain line
(B)

Understanding the Gain Line and the Tackle Line

tries (worth 4 points) means to cross the goal line and touch the ball down. You can't do that if your side is not moving forward. Going backwards or attacking the sidelines is not going forward. In backline (backfield) play, "turning the corner" should only apply to the wing when he can get to the outside of his man; otherwise, it's go forward.

Likewise, it is very difficult to win the ball from a ruck or maul by first having to go backwards. If everyone is mentally prepared and understands the necessity to go forward, then if a tackle does occur, it will be beyond the gain line or the tackle line (see fig. 1). It is so much easier for forwards to release from a scrum or line-out and move forward than have to retreat backwards to support because the backline did not move the ball forward, which brings us to the second principle: Support your forward momentum. The rugby player, coach, and spectator who understand the concepts of the gain line and the tackle line will appreciate even more the significance of the principle of Go Forward.

The Gain Line

This is an imaginary line drawn across the field of play through a platform situation: scrum, line-out, ruck, maul, penalty, and kickoff. See fig. 1 (B). The line runs from one touch line to the other. Obviously, if one crosses or penetrates the gain line by either running, handling, or kicking the ball (a short-ahead kick), then your side is moving forward and your forwards will move much faster to support when they can go forward.

Problems occur when the ball has failed to reach or penetrate the gain line. It is this condition (attacking the sidelines or moving too slowly) that forces your forward to retreat before getting involved. When a side continually fails to cross the gain line, its chances of winning are extremely diminished.

The Tackle Line

As the gain line was an imaginary line through the ball from a platform situation, so too, is the tackle line. It is the line dividing the two backlines at which point they would meet or tackle each other. See fig. 1 (C). When one backline is up on the ball or lying flat as in a defensive alignment, the tackle line advances into the opposition's half and beyond the gain line. Most times, though, the tackle line and the gain line coincide.

Support. If everyone is determined to go forward, then support comes almost naturally. After all, it's easier to run forward than to run backwards. But support is more than just forwards reinforcing at breakdown points like rucks and mauls. Support is an attitude. It also means forwards always backing up each other and backs always in position.

Support is intelligent reinforcement at critical points so that the ball never dies. It means being there in depth—not just one player but many. It also demands fitness, because if you can't get there "firstest with the mostest," then no matter what you know, you will not be able to give support. And this brings us to the third principle: Keep the Ball Alive.

Keep the Ball Alive. If your side is going forward and supporting, all is a waste of energy if the ball is constantly under a pile of bodies. Some people may think of or look for the first down indication, but it isn't going to come. If your side is not releasing the ball, then it's a penalty or worse. Failure to release the ball may cause the opposition to punish the player holding onto the ball. After all, if your side doesn't want to keep the ball moving, the other side does. They want to get their hands—or their feet—on the ball, so keep the ball moving.

One of the persistent problems with Americans starting to play rugby concerns backs who have played a lot of football. They have a tendency never to release the ball when tackled, or a desire to run through everyone. Remember the previous reference to approaching the game with the right perspective? Well, you can't expect to play good rugby if you still think football.

Keeping the ball alive also means to anticipate your support and to *make the ball available* to this support on a *continuous basis*. The ball should be made available so that many players can handle the ball—support in depth. All fifteen players in rugby can carry the ball. It is not the exclusive domain of the backs.

One last point on keeping the ball alive. If you're going forward and the ball becomes dead, then you have just neutralized your forward advantage. Yes, a scrum may develop, but why stop play? Keep the ball alive and race into the opposition, which leads to the last principle: Pressure the Opposition.

Pressure the Opposition. If you're going forward, supporting each other and keeping the ball alive, then you're exerting maximum pressure on the opposition. Why? Because your side is dictating terms. Once the opposition is under this kind of pressure, it has no choice except to defend and react to the continually changing points of pressure on the field. If these points of pressure are under your control, then the probability that the opposition can reinforce all these pressure points in exact concert with your side—or even align itself quickly enough for coverage—is very low. So, what happens? One failure on its part can create a breakthrough—and a try. Conversely, if your side is the defending side, then the application of pressure is far more critical. Since the attacking side is dictating action, you must react with greater intensity at pressure points. In short, the defending side must get the ball back. Doing this is a two-step process. First, get to the ball with more pressure than the attacking side so as to neutralize its forward advantage—hard tackling. Then, with this stronger pressure—harder rucking or better rucking, get the ball back.

The Basic Individual Skills

Rugby is a ball handling game. And everyone should know how to pick up, pass, and catch a rugby ball. One of the great features of rugby is that all fifteen players can handle the ball.

Picking Up the Ball. Sounds easy. But the rugby ball is not round and can take some funny bounces. A player who can scoop up a rugby ball while moving full speed (but under control) has a good advantage over a player who can't pick up the ball on the run.

There are five basics to picking up a rugby ball while moving.

11
Scooping up the ball

They're so simple that most players take them for granted and don't bother to learn what they are. For the record then (see photo 11):

1. Approach the ball from the side—never head on.
2. Keep your eyes on the ball.
3. Bend from the knees toward the ball.
4. Place one hand under and one hand over the ball so that the net effect enables you to scoop.
5. Drive yourself away.

It's not difficult to do in practice. The test comes in a game, when you must do it—and do it right. When the pressure's on you don't want to stumble over the ball, slow things down, or even worse, miss the ball completely. Picking up the ball should always be practiced—even for five minutes in each training session. Add pressure by having an opposition player also moving toward the ball—but at a greater distance than the man picking it up. Remember, these are drills, not contests.

The Basic Swing Pass. There are three fundamental steps involved in the swing pass:

1. *Take the ball early*. Reach for it. In almost all our sports in the United States we reach for the ball in our attempt to catch it. Rugby is no different. Don't let the ball come to you. You must go for the ball with your hands. Ideally, take the ball on the run with the opposite foot forward (see photo 12). When you're watching the ball move toward your hands, your body trunk is turned sideways toward it. At the same time your body motion is forward. In order to make the motion smooth and establish a rhythm, the foot opposite the approaching ball is forward when catching the ball.

2. *Establish control*. It's no good to reach for the ball and then to drop it or knock it forward (a knock-on offense). Use the finger tips and watch the ball move into the hands, just like an end taking a pass. And take it with the finger tips, yet with firm control. Only seals try to catch with their "palms." Catch first. Pass or run second.

3. *Release the ball*. This is the end point of the essential follow-through. Since the object of passing is quick transference of the ball, then swinging through from the take-the-ball to control-the-ball phase is almost a natural follow-through swing. In rapid-fire passing, the ball is released as the original back leg moves to a forward position and the body turns to face the player being passed to. A quick

12
Taking the ball

13
Releasing the ball

14
Short toss from the swing-pass action

one-two rhythm action (see photo 13). Remember, when you pass the ball, aim the ball in front of the receiving player and about waist high (since the player you are passing it to is at an oblique angle to you, your pass to him, though lateral and slightly back, will be forward to him). In addition, as the body trunk turns with the swinging action, the forward leg can act as a springboard from which to push off and add power and more speed to the swing pass. Some players add a snap or a flick to their swing pass by using a bit of wrist action. Sometimes a swing pass can be just a short toss (see photo 14).

One of the great assets Americans have is a high degree of manual dexterity. In most of our ball games handling the ball is the major aspect of the sport, so passing comes somewhat easy to us.

The Basic Switch Pass. This pass is really not a pass in the conventional sense, but rather a running reverse hand-off. Its purpose is to create a counteraction against the flow of traffic on the field—both from an attacking and a counterattacking situation.

One player cuts behind the ballcarrier on a scissorlike path. By turning his body the ballcarrier turns and hides the ball from his flow of action and back toward the player cutting behind him. The player cutting behind essentially takes the ball like a hand-off (see photos 15 and 16).

The original ballcarrier tries to hide his passing-the-ball action as much as possible. There are two good reasons: the first is to delay the opposition's knowledge of where the ball is going. A moment's hesitation on the part of the defender can result in a break. The second is to set up a situation for the dummy, or fake hand-off, later on. In this case the ballcarrier repeats his actions, although he does not give up the ball. If the fake-action is good, it could hold the defender for a second—enough for a break.

The Basic Loop Pass. The loop pass is the basic swing pass, but is passed back to the original passer who has looped around the man passed to. The pass is normally a short pass and is more of a little

15
Basic switch-pass from a backline attacking situation. The man passing the ball turns his body (and the ball) away from the opposition.

toss than the longer swing pass, though the action is the same. Player A passes to player B. A then loops around B and takes a short swing pass. Player A will then continue forward if his movement into the gap created an overlap. Or A will quickly swing pass the ball out and try to create an overlap somewhere else in the backline. This is an example of how your side can control and continually change pressure points in order to penetrate the gain line.

The Basic Spiral Pass. This is America's contribution to the game. And it really came to light in the early 1960s when West Point All-American football player and Rhodes scholar Peter Dawkins went to Oxford. While playing wing for Oxford he was responsible for throwing in the ball on line-outs. Dawkins threw a football spiral, thus

16
Basic switch-pass from a counterattacking situation. Fullback (or wing) moving across the field and handing off to wing (or fullback) cutting behind. It is very similar to the action on executing a reverse on a deep punt situation in football.

introducing the spiral pass. In 1968 an interview was published in *Scrumdown* magazine (now called *Rugby*) with Peter Dawkins.

We didn't really start playing around with that until the third year. The British are not eager to innovate too much in their game of rugby. But, finally, in my third year I had played a lot, and felt as though we might be able to introduce a couple of things, little twists that could make it a little more fun. In practice I'd always clown around with them and had gotten them so they could throw and catch pretty well. We sort of played touch football, which was very important to the whole procedure, because when we started out they couldn't catch a ball thrown more than ten yards. They simply couldn't catch it, had no concept of how you time a ball and catch it. So, it took a while before the backs could catch a ball. And it took a year or so of fooling around before they could throw it well. Finally, we worked up a couple of signals and decided if the time comes we'll just crank it in.

Then we tried it in a couple of games and it worked fantastically. Everyone sort of stood there and watched us as this guy went through and scored a try. So, then we began thinking in terms of the Varsity match and put it under wraps as a secret weapon. Well, the Varsity match didn't go well. We didn't win. We played very poorly. However, we did bring it out and it worked very well. It didn't win the match, but it looked good.

Since then most coaches and players have recognized its advantages. For one, the ball could be thrown farther and more accurately than with the swing pass. Inevitably, this lead to the concept of across-the-field passing. But just as an across-the-court basketball pass can be dangerous, so, too, can this sort of rugby pass. It should be done only at the right time, usually at line-outs and when counterattacking.

To throw a good and accurate spiral pass, both feet should be on the ground with the front foot pointed at the target, just as in our own football. Many good quarterbacks can throw an accurate pass on the run or in the air, but this is rugby, not gridiron. Since backline passes are all quick-action lateral type passes made on the run, throwing spirals across the pitch running flat out is very tough. In fact, you have to be made of elastic to do it right. To be truly effective the spiral has to be thrown from a relatively stopped or set position. This does not mean that a back row forward cannot pick the ball up from a set scrum, take a few steps forward to commit the opposition, and then stop to wing the ball across field to a center or wing. Before Dawkins and his spiral pass, however, no one thought of this possibility (see photo 17).

As mentioned, the spiral pass has advantages for line-out throwing. Since there is much better control—and better distance can be obtained—the spiral pass increases the chances of winning good ball (the words now are "quality possession") in the line-out. In fact, the English are now teaching all their players how to throw spiral passes, but they have labeled it the *torpedo* pass.

Another plus is that the spiral pass enables the side throwing

17
Use of the football or spiral pass in rugby. Here the number 8 has picked up, made a break, and is attempting to throw a long pass out to the backline. Trying to throw a spiral on the run is difficult. It is more effective from a set position. Note that the player passing has tried to set up in order to make a good pass.

in on a line-out to fire a long pass right out to the backline. While this is a good tactical move, it is not always a success. The United States tried a quick long pass on a line-out against England in 1977, but the English backs were ready for it. The result was an interception and a try for England. Remember, it's anyone's ball on a line-out.

Dennis Storer, UCLA rugby coach and one of the coaches of the United States team, has developed some effective tactics using the spiral pass football-style. For example, on deep kicks by the opposition, a fullback or wing taking the ball moves toward one sideline direction, stops, and then fires a pass across field to the opposite wing, who normally will be forgotten and uncovered by the kicking side. The key, though, is to make sure that everyone knows what to do (see chapter 6, Counterattack).

18
The basic screen pass technique. The first player, after picking up the ball, must attack the opposition using shoulders and back and drive forward—but always keeping the ball available. Note the leverage of the ballcarrier and how the arms are extended back to keep the ball out of reach of the opposition.

The Basic Screen Pass. This may seem confusing to Americans, since a screen pass in football means one thing while a screen pass in rugby means something different. Just think of the rugby screen as a pass made by one man shielding the ball with his body before releasing it. A screen pass is made in close quarters and usually by forwards.

The screen pass technique is the prelude to setting up the ruck or the maul, which will be discussed later. The ballcarrier drives forward with his shoulder into the tackler, knocking him forward (if possible) and simultaneously turning his back to the tackler shielding or screening the ball from both the tackler and any other opposition (see photo 18). Support must be very close to the ball-carrier because the releasing action is either:

      1. a slight flip to the closest support player, or
      2. a sort of hand-off from the hip or side if the ball-carrier cannot turn his back into the tackler, or

3. a "take" of the ball, whereby the first support player drives his shoulder into the ballcarrier and pulls the ball from him and then drives off to one side—but always forward. If this action is repeated several successive times it results in a chainlike link of players moving the ball down the field.

The Basic Spin Pass. This type of pass is principally used by the scrumhalf. It starts, of course, when the scrumhalf either gets the ball from a set scrum or a line-out situation. In such a situation, as the ball is picked up off the ground, the basic foot and body position is similar to picking up a rugby ball. The back foot is nearer the ball and the body action is a "reach and sweep" motion (see fig. 2). The front foot is pointed in the direction of the receiver, and the ball should always end up in front of the receiver (the flyhalf or stand-off). The ball is held somewhat vertical with the naturally strong hand at the top far end, or back, of the ball. The other hand is positioned under the ball and forward (see photos 19a and 19b).

In a line-out the ball will be passed to the scrumhalf so there is no picking up of the ball. But the hands, feet, and sweep action are all the same. Speed and accuracy are critical in this type of pass, not only in the ball's outgoing velocity, but in the release by the scrumhalf.

The scoop   The sweep

FIGURE 2

19a
The basic spin pass. Note the position of the hands, feet, and body.

19b
The basic spin pass, rear view

19c
The pitch-out type of pass. Instead of two hands driving the ball out, one hand is used.

Many Americans who have learned to play scrumhalf have adopted the pitchout type pass (see photo 19c). This pass is exactly like the quick pitch of a quarterback to a wide-set running back. The problem with this pass is the time it takes due to the wind-up action. A closely pursuing scrumhalf or a breakthrough forward in the line-out can get a hand on the ball or the scrumhalf as he winds up and attempts to pitch it out one-handed.

There are many ways to pass. The key is to know *when*, not *how*, to pass. The basic rule is to draw the tackle in and then move the ball out quickly. This can only be done by practicing under pressure (see drills in chapter 6).

Running

Running in rugby does not mean just running with the ball and making a few nice moves. It means the entire scope of movement about the field-of-play. And this includes moving to rucks and mauls, side stepping, swerving, or covering on a kickoff. For all these activities, running is the key. Since this is not a book on running nor on fitness per se, all commentary will be left to a few important fundamentals on how running relates to playing rugby.

According to the Rugby Football Union statistics, a match breaks down into the following running components:

1. There tend to be between 125 to 160 pieces of action, 32% of which are less than 5 seconds duration; 56% of which are less that 10 seconds duration; 85% of which are less than 15 seconds duration.

2. There are likely to be 40 set scrums; 70 rucks and mauls; 50 to 60 line-outs.

3. The average distance run per player per match is six miles. Over 50 percent of this is in short sprints.

What all this means is that the body experiences a lot of short and intense running. Couple this with the overall stamina, strength, and endurance needed for eighty minutes of play and you have two types of running: sprints and long distance. A player has to know how to run on the field. And also how to prepare his or her body to perform well. It's no fun to play when your tongue is hanging out.

Anaerobic Activity. This is essentially the maximum activity that the body can accommodate without calling in more oxygen. It's what the body can do in one burst; for example, sprinting from a set scrum to a ruck or maul. According to researchers and doctors, the maximum span of anaerobic activity is about forty seconds. After this period the body must call upon a second system, the aerobic system.

Aerobic Activity. This system uses the heart and lungs to replenish the body's demand for additional oxygen. Long distance running will condition the heart and lungs for aerobic activity—like maintaining a constant pace during the match without gasping. This is a sign of aerobic fitness. But only overloading of the anaerobic system will condition the body to sustain constant short bursts without giving up, physically and mentally.

A simple analogy between the two systems is that a sprinter, up to around three hundred yards, uses the anaerobic system. At anything above that distance, the body calls upon the aerobic system. And since 85 percent of all rugby action occurs in intervals of fifteen seconds or less, then the anaerobic system must be made fit. Concentrating on many short, intensive fitness drills is important. And if this fitness program can be linked to skill development, then training sessions will become more efficient. For example, take two packs of forwards and have them scrummage at point A, then sprint twenty yards to point B and scrummage again, then to points C, D, and E. Increase the distance to each point by five yards. Repeat this at least ten times. It's good training and forces players to push themselves as well as to concentrate. Do this at practice and watch your side improve its scrummaging and fitness.

Running with the Ball. Running with the ball involves adhering to a few guidelines:

1. If you can get past the opposition or make the break either through a fake or dummy move, or by using a burst of speed, do it. But don't run to the sidelines.

2. If you cannot get past the opposition, take the tackle in a manner that allows you to pass cleanly and accurately and keep the ball alive. If your opposite can be made to commit—and essentially take himself out of the play without having tackled you—immediately move to support the player you just passed to. Your side now has the opportunity for an overlap at the next pressure point.

3. Run with control. The ball should be held out in front (see photo 20). By holding the ball out, the side step, hip-fake or swerve, becomes more natural. Try not to carry the ball tucked under one arm when in close quarters. It's difficult to pass it this way and it will result in tying up the ball. Carry the ball almost like a loaf of bread—but out in front.

4. Get off to a fast start. Whether from a backline position, a scrum line-out, or ruck/maul situation; the first 15 meters are crucial.

20

Running with control; ball out in front, ready to pass or put a move on

Kicking

Kicking should have a purpose—either to relieve defensive pressure (a kick to touch) or to exploit an opposition weakness (a backline up too fast, for example). Players that kick aimlessly are no asset. Kicking must be practiced within the context of group or team play. Only then does the knowledge of *when* to kick develop. Kicking a rugby ball takes four basic forms: punting, cross kicking, drop kicking, and place kicking.

Punting. There is fundamentally no difference between punting a rugby ball and punting a football. The ball is held with the nose pointed somewhat down and angled away from the kicking foot. This helps insure that the instep of the kicking foot meets the curve of the ball and the spiral or screw action spin of the ball develops.

If you kick left footed, then everything is reversed. Many rugby players develop the ability to kick with either foot, which is a great advantage.

The Grubber or Chipper Kick. This is a short, almost punt-type kick that is used to keep hard-tackling backs who move up too fast "honest" or penetrate an opposition backline that is aligned too flat. The ball is dropped onto the kicking foot while on the run. The kick is usually made quite low to the ground with the instep almost vertical as it strikes the ball. The ball should shoot ahead quite low to the ground and bounce a few times so that if it does go into touch, a line-out will occur at that point (see fig. 3(a)).

Depending on the situation, the player can keep the foot more parallel to the ground and give the kick height so it drops either directly behind the oncoming backs or angles behind the opposition's scrum or line-out into an area known as "the box" (assuming a set play had initiated). This second kick is called a chipper because it falls into an area with just enough height and distance permitting the kicker's forwards to retrieve the ball and advance forward. Think of it

Chipper kick

Grubber kick

FIGURE 3a

as a baseball "Texas leaguer" just making it in, not too far and not too short, but about fifteen meters ahead.

The Cross Kick. This is a tough maneuver which calls for plenty of individual practice. The wing or outside center running flat out drops the ball, and using the *outside* leg swings it across the body toward the inside, striking the ball so that it arcs high and back in toward play and across the field.

Cross kicking is normally attempted when the attacking side is within the opposition's half and is penetrating toward the goal line. The wing may be limited to the sideline and either cannot pass the ball back into his support or is going to be tackled. Cross kicking keeps the ball alive. The high loft of the kick with its minimum forward distance enables support to get to the ball—and stay onside, of course.

The Drop Kick. This is just beautiful to see. Americans seldom drop kick when they play rugby. A good reason could be that when the drop kick was outlawed in football, the skill to do it well faded. But as rugby's popularity rises, it is evident that the skill of the drop kick is also on the rise.

The secret to good drop kicking is "good timing." Drop the ball straight and let the foot strike the ball while both body and foot are accelerating forward. The result is that the follow-through is both

Straight-on kick

Soccer-style kick

FIGURE 3b

smooth and even. Remember, with a drop kick the ball must first strike the ground.

The Place Kick. There are three uses for the place kick: the kick-off, the penalty kick-at-goal, and the conversion kick. Over the past ten or so years there has been a significant change in the place kick. Originally all place kicking, including football, was of the straight-on variety. The ball was lined up vertically with a slight tilt back toward the kicker. The kicker approached straight on, eyes on the ball with head down, and opposite foot landing a little behind the ball just prior to the kicking foot hitting the ball. And the kicking foot hit the ball slightly below the middle with a straight follow-through of the leg. The ankle must be locked with the toe of the kicking foot lifted upward.

It's still done this way, but soccer has exerted a great influence on how one can take a place kick. Just look at some of the kickers on NFL teams. Figure 3(b) shows dramatically how different the two styles are. One is really not any better than the other. It's just a matter of what feels—and works—best.

Tackling

Tackling seems to be one of the most natural skills Americans have, due to the tremendous influence of gridiron football. From the time a child of eight or nine starts in a peewee football program, through high school and college, tackling is taught and revered with almost religious fanaticism. Some American football coaches have been heard to say, "Give me eleven good tacklers and we can't lose"—which implies that the opposition can't score. But if you can't use the ball to score, well, how much fun can a scoreless tie be?

Before going into the types of tackling and the appropriate techniques, it would be wise to define a rugby tackle. According to the law, a tackle occurs when the ballcarrier is held by one or more opponents so that while he is held the *ball touches the ground*. If the ball does not touch the ground, it's not a tackle. Even if the player is on the ground and on his back, he can still pass the ball. Remember also that a tackled player must release the ball in rugby or it's a penalty. This is quite different from an American football tackle, where all that is needed is to stop the ballcarrier's forward progress (the ball does not have to touch the ground). Even if one knee just grazes the ground it is ruled a tackle. In addition, the ballcarrier in gridiron never, never releases the ball when tackled. These two differences in tackling have to be understood in order to play rugby properly. Remember, approach the game with the right perspective. Also, when you are in a situation such as a one-on-two, you must always commit to the man with the ball and tackle him. If you play the ball and he dummies and leaves you standing, it's your fault. If you tackle the ballcarrier and he passes to his teammate, you did your job.

It's not unusual to see many Americans new to the game play rugby and forget to release the ball or try to bull through for extra yardage when it doesn't mean anything. Remember, in Rugby Union continuous possession is only maintained when the ball is kept alive. Therefore, when you tackle the ballcarrier you must be sure of two things:

1. The ballcarrier cannot release the ball to his support *if the ball has not touched the ground*; and
2. The ballcarrier is taken down quickly so that the ball will immediately touch the ground *and be released*.

The Front Tackle. The technique here is almost like a football tackle except for one *big* difference. You *do not* aim or butt your head into the ballcarrier's breastbone. You don't have a helmet on, and

21

A perfect front tackle. Note the head position to one side, shoulder into mid-section, and firm wrapping of the arms (United States vs. France).

---

there is a very good chance of serious neck injury if you still cling to the old dictum of "butt 'em." The ballcarrier is moving at full speed toward you with the objective of either taking the tackle with his shoulder and back so he can release the ball out to his support, or to put a move on. Consequently, the tackling position is similar to football with the solid base and eyes focused on the midsection. Your forward momentum may not be as great as that of the ballcarrier, so any head action into the ballcarrier is going to be very dangerous.

In making the front tackle, the following technique is used (see photo 21):

1. Aim the head to one side and drive the shoulder into the ballcarrier's lower midsection or thighs, wrapping your arms around the legs.

2. Let the ballcarrier's momentum carry him forward and you backward.

3. As you fall backward, turn so that you end up on top.

22

After the front tackle, turn and end up on top of the ballcarrier.

This can prevent him from releasing the ball if it did not touch the ground (see photo 22).

4. Never let go until the ballcarrier is tackled, then get up immediately and move to the ball. Do not lie on the ballcarrier nor on the ground.

The Side Tackle. Again the side tackle in rugby is similar to the side tackle in football with one *big* difference. You do not aim your head in front of the ballcarrier. Your head is aimed so that is ends up on or below the backside of the ballcarrier. The technique is as follows (see photo 23):

1. Aim the head behind the ballcarrier with the shoulder driving into a position between the thighs and the waist.

2. Wrap your arms tightly around the ballcarrier. If he's big slide down to the legs. No player can run if both legs are held firmly.

3. As you fall, turn so you end up on top.

The Smother Tackle. This is a "hug" tackle and is designed to prevent the ballcarrier from both moving forward and from passing

23
The side tackle. Note the head position and tightly wrapped arms.

the ball. This type of tackle is most often used where an obvious one-on-one situation exists and the defending player cannot make a low tackle. An example would be a fullback trying to contain a ballcarrier who has made a break and is on his way for a try. A front or a side tackle would allow the ballcarrier to score (if the try line was very close) or allow the ballcarrier to pass off to his support. The technique is as follows (see photo 24a):

    1. Move into the ballcarrier from a high position with the shoulders and chest striking the ballcarrier's chest.
    2. Wrap the arms around the ballcarrier so he cannot pass the ball—use a bear hug.
    3. Drive forward so he cannot move forward.

Sometimes this tackle necessitates moving into the ballcarrier with full force. Such a tackle is a straight-on tackle following the basic front tackle technique (see photo 24b). The big difference is that forward impact takes both man and ball immediately to the

24a
The smother tackle. Note the "bear-hug" position and arms preventing the ballcarrier from passing.

24b
The "crash" tackle, taking the man and the ball to the turf.

ground. This type of tackle is called a crash tackle, and most Americans have been doing it without a second thought.

The Rear Tackle. The cardinal rule here is don't leap too early or you'll catch the ballcarrier's heel in your face. The basic technique is as follows:

1. When approaching the ballcarrier from behind, reach for the waist or hips and encircle him.

2. Let the arms slide down to the thighs and hold on very tightly. As the ballcarrier falls forward, slide down to the legs and maintain a death grip. If you don't you may still get kicked.

3. When the ballcarrier falls forward and the ball touches the ground, get up quickly.

3

FUNDAMENTALS OF FORWARD PLAY – THE RUCK AND THE MAUL

Who Are the Forwards?

There are eight forwards on a rugby team. They are conceptually divided into two groups. The first is the front five: the loose head prop (left side of the front row), the hooker, the tight head prop (right side of the front row), and the two second row locks. The second group is the back row: two flankers or wing forwards and the number 8.

For many years, especially here in the U.S., forwards were perceived and considered to be football "linemen" and really not part of the attack. Back row forwards were chosen for their ability to just play linebacker. Now, however, the back row is viewed as a vital link between the chain of forwards and the backline. The use of the back row as an attacking unit is becoming more and more apparent—especially when more pressure per square foot is wanted at the breakdown point or an attacking point. Such uses as the number 8 pick from a set scrum and quick-pass out to the scrumhalf to set up and overlap; or even winging a long pass out to the center or wing after a pickup is becoming more and more popular.

Forwards must be mobile and ball hungry. You cannot win

rugby matches with forwards who can't move, or don't enjoy body contact.

The pack of forwards must be, to quote some football coach, "hostile, agile, and mobile"—a virtual blanket of moving players linked together by the same two powerful objectives: get the ball and keep the ball.

These two objectives dovetail with the four principles of play discussed earlier: Go Forward, Support, Keep the Ball Alive, and Pressure the Opposition.

Contact and Support — the Basis for the Ruck and the Maul

The ruck and the maul are very important in setting the mood of the game for forwards. To form a ruck or a maul players must make contact and support each other. This contact and support lead to an attitude of oneness, like that big moving blanket.

The ruck and the maul are nothing more than moving platforms of attack. The line-out and the scrum are stationary platforms of attack. Think of a ruck or a maul as a moving scrum where your side must get more pressure (either more players or better rucking or mauling technique) to the breakdown point before the opposition. Only then will your side maintain forward drive and possession.

The Maul. A maul can take place only on the field of play, never in the in-goal area, and is formed by one or more players from each side on their feet and in physical contact closing around a player who is carrying the ball (see photo 18). A maul ends when the ball goes onto the ground, is passed out, or when a player emerges with it or it becomes a stalemate and the referee orders a scrum.

When do you form a maul? When the ball is on the ground and you can get to the ball, pick it up and move forward. When a ball is loose (for example, a tackled player has released it), move in quickly, pick up the ball—and if the opposition is there a second or so later, a maul will form. In forming the maul, *always* remember that the ball *must* be available to your support. Too many players run smack into the opposition and never remember to keep the ball available.

The technique in forming a maul is not hard to master. It starts out like the basic screen pass. Move into the opposition driving forward, staying low, and using the shoulders and back. As you drive forward extend the arms back holding the ball away from the opposition and making it visible to your support.

The first supporting player (see photo 25) reaching the ball-carrier *must* come in on the "ball available side." The critical move is for him to come into his teammate hard and low turning *the outside shoulder in* and literally tearing the ball out of his hands. The support player then turns toward the additional support that is just arriving.

The arriving support must use their eyes to see what's happening. To pack blindly into a maul is foolish. It just kills an effective platform and neutralizes forward momentum. The second supporting player arriving at the maul *must pack* to the new ball available side or opposite side of the maul (see photos 26a and 26b). The next wave of supporting players—because by now support should be arriving in waves of two or three players—must alternately pack to balance the maul. If balanced packing is not achieved, then a wheel of the maul might develop.

As the maul is forming, each arriving player must drive low to maintain forward momentum—to keep going toward their goal line. The maul should have no gaps. All members must be bound tightly. Generally, you want to drive the ruck parallel to the side lines. At the right command the ball is released to the scrumhalf. Packing into the maul should be hard, fast, and quick. It's not a time to rest. The maul and the ruck are just temporary pauses in a team's rapid forward drive. As soon as the ball is out, it's on to the next pressure point.

The Ruck. The ruck is another moving platform. It, too, can only take place on the field of play. A ruck is formed when the ball is on the ground and one or more players from each side are on their feet and in physical contact, closing around the ball between them. As a point to remember, when the ball is placed on the ground in a maul it automatically becomes a ruck.

25
The first supporting player *must* come in on the "ball available" side, driving the outside shoulder into the ballcarrier's chest and shielding the ball.

When do you form a ruck? If you can get to the breakdown point first but cannot pick up the ball, then a ruck will form. Successful rucks occur when players cannot pick up the ball or make it cleanly available, yet want to maintain possession and forward momentum.

The steps are very similar to the maul except the feet, instead of the hands, are used to help make the ball available. Assume that the player on the ground in photo 27 has just been tackled. The supporting players must get to this breakdown point first and put feet and body over man and ball. One player should not be there alone. There should be at least two initiating the ruck. One player can be driven back by more opposition support.

The following waves of support must come into the ruck low and hard making shoulder contact and constantly driving forward over man and ball (see photos 28–31). In both the ruck and the maul the essential driving position is almost the same as a football lineman after the initial contact on the line of scrimmage against a defending lineman. Stay low and drive. In addition, here's a little

26a

The first supporting player, after tearing the ball from the ball-carrier, turns in toward his support. The second supporting player (right side) *must* come in on the new "ball available" or opposite side of the maul.

26b

Successive supporting players pack in alternately on opposite sides of the maul. Every player must continually drive forward so that the maul is moving forward.

27
The first two players to reach the breakdown point bind and go in together, low and driving forward.

rule players should remember when rucking: Always take a friend to a ruck. Never go solo if you can help it. Grab someone and go in like a blanket.

As the packing swells, the steps are like the maul. Depending on where the ruck takes place, the first support should go to the ruck's far side. The next support takes the near or opposite side. Again, this is not a static situation, but rather a moving one with the ruck always going forward over the ball. Remember, the same offside line is created in a ruck, maul, or scrum, that is, the hindmost foot of the last player determines the offside line. So if you move the ruck forward, keeping the ball inside, you drive the offside line forward and the opposition must retreat.

The Hand Ruck. The hand ruck, a misnomer since hands are never allowed to handle the ball on the ground or in a ruck, is basically a maul in which the ball has been put on the ground either by the initial player picking up the ball and starting the maul, or by the support player who took the ball. Sometimes the opposition may have obtained a hand on the ball, whereby it is

28
The successive waves of support join the ruck, packing to the far side first (away from the open side of the field). Players joining a ruck must try to come into the ruck in pairs in order to add momentum and drive it forward.

29
The packing in the ruck is like a moving scrum with tight binding—a continuous driving shove forward using the feet to play the ball (if necessary).

30
A back view of the ruck. Note the hands and arms binding and the legs all in a driving position.

31
A side view of the ruck

32

A successful maul. Note the two close supporting players and
how tightly they bind and shield the player with the ball. The
player passing out the ball originally took the ball from the man
with the taped wrist. This play initiated the maul. The passing out
of the ball concludes the maul.

almost impossible to pass it out. The best move is to force the ball to the ground and ruck, using the feet to move the ball back to the scrumhalf.

Is There a Guide to When You Ruck and When You Maul? Time and space are the key factors. A player must be able to recognize what time-and-space situation dictates forming a ruck versus a maul.

A basic guide is that if the opposition is closing in on the ball and space between him or her, the ball, and you is such that you will reach the ball in time to pick it up first, then scoop it up, go over the tackled player, and either form the maul with the oncoming opposition or pass it out immediately. On the other hand, if the oppostion is close, then the first player (preferably two players) to the ball from your side should step over the ball and initiate the ruck.

FIGURE 4

Resultant Driving Forces

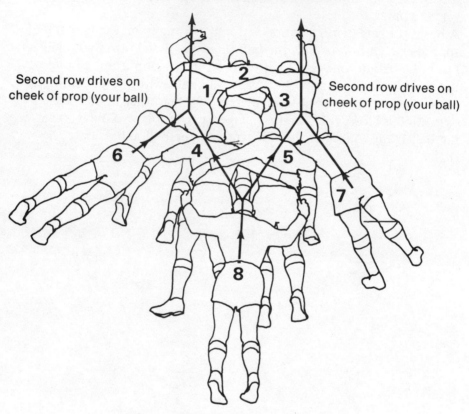

Second row drives on cheek of prop (your ball)

Second row drives on cheek of prop (your ball)

The Physics of Scrummaging

4

FUNDAMENTALS OF FORWARD PLAY — SCRUMMAGING

Probably no other aspect of play engenders the image of rugby like the set scrum, with bodies massed together in a melange of pushing and shoving. But there's a science to scrummaging, and the side that knows the basics and puts them to work will most surely win the ball—and more.

According to the laws, to form a scrummage all one side needs is the front row: two props on the outside and a hooker in the middle. After this you can have as many players as you want in the scrum, although it is advisable just to keep the normal eight. If you pack with more than eight, the opposition will always have an extra man in the backline, and it's tough to cover an open player from a set scrum.

Scrummaging techniques have changed in the last decade. Following are tested techniques that integrate players successfully, resulting in effective scrummaging. Coaches and players should take this information as a guide and select as well as refine techniques for their personnel.

The front row is the key to scrummaging. If your front row is not solid, then chances are your scrummaging will not be effective. The physics behind scrummaging are quite straightforward (see fig. 4). As you can see, the resultant force is a for-

FIGURE 5

Suggested Foot Positioning

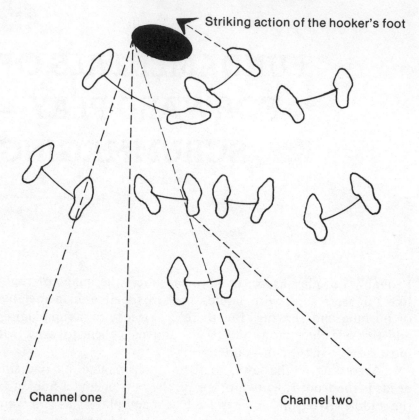

Striking action of the hooker's foot

Channel one

Channel two

ward drive. Notice that the wing forwards are heavily involved in the push. For many years the wing forwards were considered line-backers who were just appendages to the scrum and did not really provide any drive. Now, however, the second row and the wing forwards shove equally hard and form the middle power linkage of the 3–4–1 scrum formation.

Good scrummaging starts with correct foot positioning. If the feet are wrong, then everything else can fall apart and break down (see fig. 5). The feet are positioned to provide the maximum base and driving force. Note the difference in the foot position of the two front row props.

But scrummaging only starts with the feet. There are other equally critical aspects to good scrummaging which all have to be done in harmony. The four notes that give that perfect harmony are:

1. FOOT POSITION. This establishes the base.
2. LEGS AND BACK POSITION. This establishes the drive.
3. ARM POSITION. This establishes the bind.
4. HEAD POSITION. This establishes the direction of your body.

The Front Row

Note the foot position (see photo 33). The loose head prop (on the right, blond hair) has his right foot behind the hooker. The

33
A good front row starts with the right foot position.

34

The next critical step in a good front row is proper binding.

tight head prop is almost flush with the hooker and tries to keep his hip as close to the hooker as possible.

The hooker binds over both props' shoulders and grabs their jerseys under the armpits (see photo 34). The loose head (number 1) always binds first, that is, under the tight head's arm. This is to help support the hooker as he shifts his body and legs toward the ball in the set position. Some hookers bind under their props' arms. Others go under the loose head and over the tight head (see fig. 6). It's a matter of what feels best. The safest and most widely used position is the over-both style. Again look at the loose head's right foot.

FIGURE 6

Binding Techniques

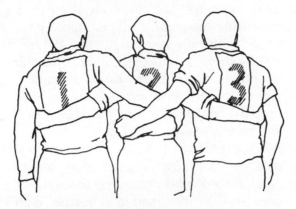

(A) The under-both technique

(B) The over-both technique

(C) The under-over technique

The next step is the down position (see photos 35a and 35b). Note several things. First, how the hooker has shifted his body so that the striking foot (right foot) will be closer to the ball. The hooker essentially wants to "lay" his body along the tunnel. The hooker is almost using the right leg of the loose head prop as a support, although technically he cannot, since the law states that the hooker must be in a "pushing" position. But many hookers can assume this stance and still be in a pushing position.

Second, the tight head now drops his foot back a bit and drives his hip into the hooker. It's almost a weld of the two hips as the hooker shifts his body toward the ball.

Third, look at the backs of the two props—both straight and solid, like a table top. The loose head is a bit higher, and this is as it should be since the hooker needs a tunnel to see the ball.

Finally, note the legs—bent and in a shoving position to snap and drive forward. The legs and bent knees should always be behind the hips.

The Loose Head Prop

The basic job of the loose head prop is to keep that tunnel open and not to be taken down. If the loose head drops his head, his back will follow, bend easily, and he'll go down, thereby closing the tunnel. If the loose head is forced too low, the hooker cannot see nor even strike. No matter what the opposite tight head does, the loose head (so called because his head is outside the scrum and closest to the scrumhalf) must never lose his cool or be intimidated. He or she is the pillar of the scrum.

To help, the loose head must have a few good physical tools. One of the most important is a very strong left arm. Since the opposite tight head has his arm outside the loose head's, the loose head must never let that left arm be bent down. It must be as parallel to the ground as possible. One method to help establish a parallel arm position is to grab the opposite tight head's jersey quickly in the hollow of his back as the scrums come together and hold. Another move is to reach out quickly and grab the top of the opposite tight head's shorts, holding the arm parallel and never letting the tight head leverage his arm to a pressure position. One

35a
Getting into the correct and most comfortable down position is very important (back view).

35b
The down position (front view)

final point: The loose head always places the top of his head into the breastbone of the tight head. This all occurs as the two sides engage for a scrum.

The Tight Head Prop

On the tight head side of the attacking scrum, don't worry about bending your opposite into the ground. So many tight heads try to bend their opposite on their own ball-in that they forget the two most critical things, driving and supporting the hooker with the left hip. It is far more important to drive and support than to try to look strong. Remember, the most probable tactic the opposition will use against your ball-in is an eight-man shove. If the tight head gets involved with a personal battle, then it's six men against eight. Even if you win the strike, their extra man may be enough to push your scrum back and give you a bad ball. When it's their ball, that's the time to pressure the loose head into the sod.

On the opposition's ball-in, the tight head must try to minimize the view of the opposite hooker by forcing his opposite loose head down. Since it's his main task to keep the tight head neutralized and support his hooker, the result is usually a standoff. The best move then is either the eight-man shove or a strike against the head. In the case of the strike against the head, the hooker shifts his body as near the tight head as possible and strikes at the ball with the near foot. In this case it is also the right foot. The tight head then assists the hooker by using his outside foot to sweep the ball back. It is a two-man maneuver, hooker striking and prop sweeping. This is the only time a prop assists in hooking the ball.

The Second Row

The next link to the scrum is the second row or lock forwards (see photo 36). The two second rows bind into the scrum with their heads between the props and the hooker. Note that even with the loose head's right foot back, the second row player can get his head in the gap. There's space—you just have to find it.

36
The next link to the scrum is incorporating the second row.

The outside arm comes under the prop's legs and grabs onto the top of the shorts or onto a piece of the jersey. It depends on your reach and what feels best. But don't grab their legs. Look also at the second row's legs (see photo 37). Coming into the scrum the outside legs are forward and the inside legs are back. In this case, since it is a setup, the knees are down. Normally, the knees would be off the ground and getting ready for the drive position.

The feet establish the base position. The hips of both second row forwards are in front of their knees. The hips of the second row are always lower than the hips of the props. This lower hip position results in the legs and knees closer to the ground. This low hip-knee-leg stance is the basis for the snap-shove-drive action in the scrummaging.

37
Proper binding in the second row and correct foot position make for a solid and powerful scrum. Note also the second row concentrating the drive on the cheek of the prop.

The binding in the second row is also very critical. When it is your ball-in, both second rows drive below the inside cheeks of their props (refer to fig. 4). Since the drive is concentrated on the props, the arm bind between the two second rows should be lower to allow the outside shoulders room to drive in and below the prop's buttocks. This is the basis for the seven-man shove. When it's an eight-man shove, the hooker is involved and the drive of the two second rows can be channeled straight ahead. One shoulder goes below the prop's buttocks, and the other shoulder goes below the hooker's. To establish a tighter bind, with more concentrated forward drive, the two second rows should bind higher—almost at the shoulders.

The drive from the second row is exactly like a driving

position in football—low and moving ahead with short, choppy steps. The real key is the initial snap-shove that must come as the ball is put into the tunnel and the hooker strikes. It's like Newton's law: A body in motion tends to stay in motion. Once you have the initial shove won and gained momentum, it's easier to push the opposition backwards.

The Back Row

The final linking of the scrum is with the back row (see photos 38a and 38b). The three back row players bind in as follows: The two wing forwards drive their shoulders under the buttocks of the two props, the number 8 packs in with his head between the two second rows binding over their outside legs. This binding must be tight. But it must not impede the drive of the second row. The number 8 must aid in the shove, and also control the scrum so it does not turn or wheel out of control (more on wheeling later). Notice also that the number 8 is very low, hips forward of the bent knees and in a driving position.

38a
The final link in the scrum is the back row. Note the forty-five degree driving position of the wing forwards. Number 8 has the lowest hip position in the scrum.

38b
A side view of the scrum. Note the half-pyramid structure.

39
A contrast in
basic scrummaging

Take a look at photo 39. Look at the team with the black jerseys. This is how the proper scrum alignment should look—a half-pyramid. The front row is the highest, the second row and wing forwards a level lower, and the number 8 on the lowest. Note their pyramid structure and the wing forward pushing inward as well as forward on the prop. The scrum with the light jerseys is off-balance. Look at the near side second row. He is much too high and, in fact, is pushing more downward than forward. The number 8 also has his hips too high and therefore is not able to provide maximum driving power.

When one level or link in the scrum gets higher than the level in front, scrummage drive and control diminishes. When this situation becomes acute and in a state of imbalance, one player could pop out of the scrum or it could collapse. Always remember to keep the back straight, knees bent, and head up. If trouble occurs, the first move should be to drop the hips.

Striking and Channeling the Ball

Before finishing with the scrum, these two very important aspects of scrummaging should be explained. We'll start with channeling. There are two channels for the ball in the scrum (refer to

fig. 5). Channel one ball is for fast and clean ball to the scrum-half. The strike by the hooker is quick and the movement is a sweep of the ball back as the scrum snap-shoves and drives forward. As you can see, the ball must be swept between the loose head's legs and move back between the wing forward and the second row. Channel one ball puts the maximum pressure on the scrumhalf.

The second row and wing forward must never—no, never—kick the ball back. The forward drive of the scrum coupled with the hooker's strike-and-sweep will provide the momentum for getting the ball back.

Channel two ball is more difficult for the forwards because it is more controlled ball. Most times it is guided back by the second row and the number 8 as the scrum drives forward. Channel two ball is used in such situations as pushing the ball over for a score where the number 8 touches the ball down as soon as it crosses the goal line. Another situation is for a number 8 pickup to start on attack.

Of course, if the strike is bad, given everything else, the chances of getting good ball reduce dramatically. In rugby, the basis for attack rests on the assumption that your side will win its own ball. If your side cannot win its own ball, then chances of scoring drop. And striking for the ball is important in winning not only your ball but clean ball.

To start with, the hooker must be in a comfortable position—secure and able to move body and foot to strike at the ball (refer to photos 26a and 26b). He or she should let the props take the scrum as low as possible, yet still be able to strike. If your hooker can strike and sweep at a lower scrum position than the opposition, its hooker is in trouble. He will not be able to get his feet off the ground and strike. Look at the twist of the hooker's body to allow the striking foot to move close to the tunnel opening. The hooker strikes with the right, or far, foot. While some may say the near foot is closer, the result is less control on the strike-and-sweep action.

Many hookers use a signal with the scrumhalf indicating when to put the ball in. Opening the left hand or squeezing the left hand is such a signal. The loose head must be very sensitive to this hand signal because as the ball is put-in, the loose head must drive up as well as forward, insuring that the hooker can see and strike the ball. It needs timing and takes practice. In addition, everyone in the scrum, especially the second rows and the wing forwards, must be looking at that ball.

The Eight-Man Shove Versus the Seven-Man Shove

When it's your put-in, your scrum is essentially in a seven-man shoving situation. The hooker is not involved in the shove. All driving effort is transmitted through the props. The action is snap-shove-drive.

On the other hand, when the opposition is putting in the ball, the best defensive move is to use all eight men and shove. The action is still snap-shove-drive, but now the forward push is also transmitted to the hooker. The second row uses both shoulders and divides its driving force equally below the prop's buttocks and the hooker's buttocks.

To deal with an eight-man shove is not difficult if the scrum members quickly recognize that such a tactic is being used against them. For starters, the attacking side must put the ball in fast and snap-shove quickly in order to establish that degree of forward momentum. If the call is to keep the ball in the scrum for a pushover or a number 8 pick up, then the props and the second row must lock their knees in this forward snap position with the legs straight, hips forward, and backs as flat as table tops for leverage. The net effect is that the eight-man shove is confronted with an opposing force that has better leverage and cannot be forced backwards easily. The attacking scrum members are locked into a forward shoving position. The only way such a scrum will go backwards is if the opposing eight men drive them back all together, locked in position with their feet churning the ground like a plow.

Wheeling

The fundamentals of wheeling the scrum are quite simple. Doing it correctly and at the right time, however, are more difficult tasks.

Since wheeling is a more sophisticated scrummaging maneuver, and this book is a primer, only two wheeling moves will be explained.

Wheeling the scrum is to turn the scrum using your loose head prop as the fulcrum. Wheeling action is clockwise and can be done on your put-in as well as theirs. The physics first involve your tight head driving forward, then stepping backward, taking the opposition loose head with him. Since the opposition is already driving forward, the loose head will readily move forward toward the tight head. The other members of the pack use their left shoulders and concentrate on driving to the left. The scrum will then turn or wheel left rotating about your loose head.

Wheeling to the open side (strong side). The objective of the wheel is to turn your scrum and outflank the opposition back row. Your back row is closer to the open side gain line, and their back row is away from the open side (see fig. 7(A)). When wheeling to the open side the ball should be channel two ball. The number 8 picks up and starts around the scrum. Your scrumhalf has retreated and comes into a backline in order to take a pass. The blind side wing forward must follow the number 8 because the number 8 will be stopped by the opposition wing forward (the first man around the scrum with the ball is the responsibility of the defending wing forward, the second player the responsibility of the number 8). The number 8 quickly passes out to the supporting wing forward who will either look for a break or, more likely, move the ball out to the now supporting scrumhalf. The result is an extra man in the backline because the opposition scrumhalf will not be able to recover quickly enough as his opposite has moved out to a backline position. Defensively, the wing forward taking the ball from the number 8 should be covered by the opposition number 8.

Wheeling to the blind side (weak side). Here also, ball out of the scrum should be channel two ball. The number 8 picks up the ball and most probably will be stopped by the opposition wing forward. Support is provided by your blind side wing forward and the scrumhalf coming around the back of the scrum. A move like this should be done close to the opposition's goal line (see fig. 7(B)).

FIGURE 7

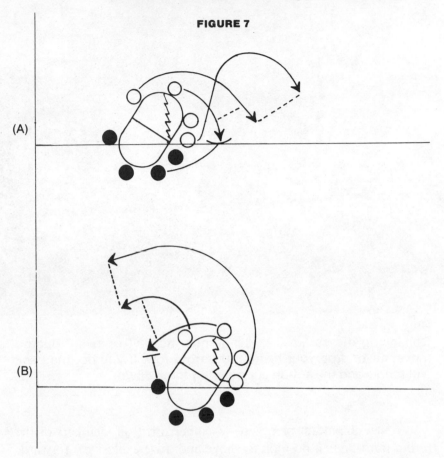

(A)

(B)

Stopping a wheel. To stop a wheeling move, two methods are used. The first method is the safest and the best. It's called crabbing. As the opposition scrum starts to wheel, step into the direction of the wheel, or to your right. Remember, they are going to use their loose head as the fulcrum. This stepping or crabbing action neutralizes the rotation.

The second method is very dangerous and should never be used. It's performed by collapsing the scrum. When a scrum is collapsed, both hookers are in a very vulnerable and dangerous situation which can easily damage shoulders and neck. In fact, the entire front row is in jeopardy when the scrum collapses (see photo 40). Playing rugby is for enjoyment. Pyrrhic victories are for fools or worse.

40

Collapsing the scrum is a dangerous move. To prevent such a move, never drop your head in the front row. If you do, the back will follow and the action is a bending force down.

A few important points to remember: first, all members of the scrum must be in a position to shove and drive explosively forward. The only exception is the hooker on your ball-in. Keep proper foot position, knees bent and legs in a driving position, hips forward, all set for snap-shove-drive and all packed together with iron-clad binding. The net result is a powerful drive forward transmitted through the backs of each linking row, all under control. The channels must be open for clean ball, and the hooker must strike in a flash.

1. The foot position establishes the base.
2. Legs, knees, and back positions establish the drive.
3. Arm position establishes the bind.
4. Head position establishes direction.

5

FUNDAMENTALS OF FORWARD PLAY — THE LINE-OUT

The line-out can resemble the basketball tap play. Player position in the scrum does not fix position in the line-out. Players should be positioned according to their capabilities. It is useless to put the number 8 as the last man if that player is the best jumper. If the hooker can't pass the ball, use another forward—a prop or a wing forward— whoever can do it best.

The basic guidelines are to position the two best jumpers at the number two and number four spots (see fig. 8(A)). The fastest forward should always be the last player in the line-out. Next to the two jumpers should be two solid and dependable supporting players. Usually it's a prop at one and another prop at three. But it could be a wing forward. It depends on how the personnel adapt to line-out play. Don't be locked into formulas.

A line-out is formed when at least two players from each side line up in a single line parallel to each other and face the touch line. Each player must stand at least one meter from his teammate and a half-meter from the opposition line. The first player in the line-out cannot be closer than five meters to the touch line. The last man cannot be farther than fifteen meters from the touch line. And the side that is throwing the ball in sets the length of the line-out: The last man of the defending side must be inside the last man of the throwing side.

The line-out has three fundamental parts:

1. the pass or throw-in;
2. the reception or catch of the ball;
3. the support, or formation of a moving wall.

FIGURE 8

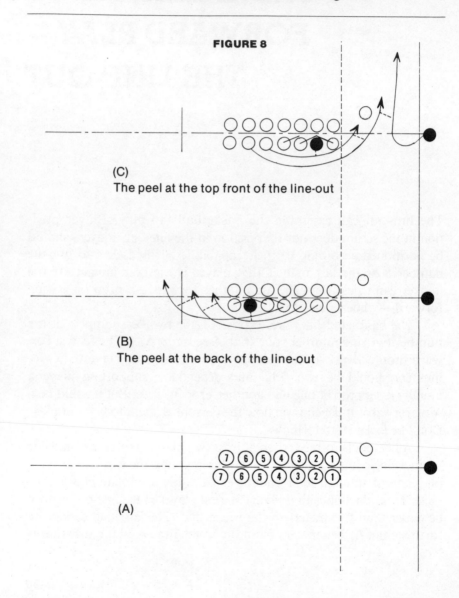

(C)
The peel at the top front of the line-out

(B)
The peel at the back of the line-out

(A)

The Passing of the Ball

As scrummaging begins with a good front row, so the line-out starts with a good passer. If you don't have a good passer, one who can throw the ball accurately, then find one or develop one. As a good hooker is proud of his striking, so should the passer be proud of his line-out passing. Little thought and practice is usually given to line-out play, especially to the passer. They're like afterthoughts. In fact, the line-out is a better platform to attack since the scrumhalf and the entire backline have more time and space in which to set up. If the ball is just thrown with a "wing and a prayer" attitude, then line-out play will be nothing more than a roll of the dice—and those odds are not good for winning rugby matches.

The best type of pass is the spiral pass. It's easy to throw and offers the options of distance and accuracy. The British, French, New Zealanders, and others do not have the scope of ball handling games that we do. Throwing and catching a ball is, pardon the expression, our "cup of tea." All the other styles of throwing are due to an inability to pass and should be discarded. Let's use what we do best.

Catching the Ball

Catching the ball is the next critical step. It's just like jumping for a rebound in basketball or grabbing a high pass in football. There's no secret to it. It's a matter of timing. Timing between passer and receiver (see photo 41). Sometimes a jumper can take a step forward as the ball is thrown and then leap up and backward. The tactic here is that the step forward is a faking move influencing the opposite jumper also to go forward. The actual jump, though, is up and back, taking a loblike pass. The variation to this is to fake backwards and then leap up and forward and take a harder pass in front of the opposition jumper. Other variations to these two moves may be worked out in practice. Tapping is another tactic which will be discussed shortly.

One point that should be brought out is that of signals. The passer, the jumper, and the scrumhalf must all know in advance who is to receive the ball. A signal system is usually worked out between

41
Catching the ball in the line-out

the scrumhalf and the forwards. Some use the foot positions of the scrumhalf to indicate who will get the ball. And others use a verbal signal barked out by the scrumhalf. In any respect, every forward must know who the ball will be passed to so the proper supporting action occurs. The passer and the jumper then time their actions.

Supporting the Jumper

If the pass is accurate, the ball caught and taken down, then support must be quick, solid, and dependable. If not, the opposition will penetrate the support wall and either knock the ball out of the jumper's hands, grab and turn the jumper around toward their side and take the ball, or burst through and pounce on the scrumhalf as he receives the ball. Support is very, very vital.

Winning a Line-out

Assuming that the throw is good, the number two jumper in this situation (see photo 42) catches the ball, takes it down, and turns

42
The number 2 jumper catching the ball

43
Forming the wall of support in the line-out

toward his scrumhalf. The forwards in the line-out immediately start to form a wall to support the jumper and protect the ball. The two closest supporting players to the jumper step forward with the foot nearest him or her and begin to bind (see photo 43). The action is similar to forming a ruck or a maul. The difference is that in the initial stage these two support players bind over the jumper's back. This is recommended because it reduces the chances of knocking the ball as the jumper takes it down.

Some players prefer to bind inside (see fig. 9). It all depends on what works best. As the wall forms the other supporting players bind in and essentially form a maul. And with a maul, always drive forward and bind strongly (the maul is a forward moving wall). It's just like a maul from loose play, only in this case, the maul is formed from a set situation. If the jumper had been at number four position, which is the safest position to pass to, then this player would have three supporting players on each side. Remember, the line-out starts as soon as the ball leaves the passer's hand.

Variation in the Line-Out

The objective of the line-out is to gain possession of the ball and use it for a platform of attack. The line-out, as compared to the

FIGURE 9
Inside binding on the line-out

scrum, does offer a lot of opportunity to vary the attack. The ball can be thrown to any player in the line-out or to the backline. The best to throw to are the number two, the number four, the number six, the last man, and sometimes the number one. There are also variations in how each of these players can take the ball—a catch or a tap.

The Tap Play

Sometimes it is advisable to jump, and instead of catching the ball, touch-tap it directly to the scrumhalf (see photo 44). It's a good move for getting the ball quickly back and out of the line-out, but it's dangerous if executed poorly. A loose ball bouncing around can cause two problems that have to be overcome: regaining possession and mounting an attack. In addition, the loss of good ball causes momen-

44
The tap play at number 4 directly to the scrumhalf. Note how number 5 has moved across the gain line and sealed off the opposite jumper at 4.

---

tary breakdowns by the side throwing-in. Forwards are looking to give support up front, and instead the ball is bouncing around behind them. In such a situation there are proper coverage responsibilities. For instance, if the ball is tapped and it is loose or uncontrolled in the front area of the line-out, it is the responsibility of number 5 or 6 to move back to front and try to clean up the situation. If the ball is tapped back toward the end of the line-out, it is the passer who must clean up at number 4 or number 6 position. This rule applies for any ball that is supposed to be taken or tapped, but gets loose.

A tap play can also be used from the number one position. This play has to be based on the ability of this first man. For one thing, he must have good hands: The ball must be passed hard, straight, and at about the height of the number one player's normally extended reach. The number one jumps up and forward as the ball is thrown and with the inside hand tap-swishes it to the scrumhalf who has moved toward the front of the line-out to be in a better receiving position.

The Peel at the Back

The peel is another variation and can start at either end of the line-out. The more effective place is the back with a peel at number 6, although a peel at number 2 is good when close to the opposition's goal line.

The peel at the back of the line-out starts with the number 6 player. The ball is passed high and rather straight, enabling the player at six to leap up and soft-tap it down. The position of the jumper in photo 44 shows the correct moves. Simultaneously, the numbers 3, 2, and 4 release from the line-out in that order and parallel it. The number 3 takes the soft-tap down from the number 6. The number 3 should be right next to the jumper. After catching it, the number 3 races past the last player and corner-flags. The number 2 is right on his heels followed by the number 4 (see photo 45). Note in Fig. 8(B) that the numbers 5 and 7 stay in to bind. After the tap, they should release and support. The entire support action in the peel is for each man to act as a link in a chain taking the ball forward—but not all in the same area.

45

Number 3 has just taken a tap and is starting to turn upfield after passing the last player in the line-out (in striped jersey and white headband). Numbers 2 and 4 are right on his heels to support.

After the number 3 starts to corner-flag, the opposition's last man will more than likely tackle him. The key is to have the second two players there to reinforce in depth at that moment. If 2 and 4 are there on the button, then screen passing the ball is easy and forward momentum is maintained. The back peel has to be quick and very intense so that the gain line is penetrated quickly.

Inside support now comes from the remaining forwards. The last thing you want is a linking movement running to the opposite touch line. The number 4 player or last player in the peel should look to either pass directly inside (a short toss) or screen pass to the inside, causing the chain of support to roll inside.

The Peel at the Front

The best time to use this move is within the opposition's twenty-two-meter line. The ball is passed high and hard to number two, who taps down to number 5. Number 6 is the first supporting player, followed by the passer. As soon as 5 has taken the ball, movement is directly upfield and toward the goal line. Remember, the touch line is very close. Other forwards support by going directly forward. The supporting passing action this time is outside. Note in Figure 8 (C) that numbers 3, 4, and 1 all bind on 2.

Short Line-Outs

The law states that you need just two players from each side to form the line-out. Starting from this, a line-out can be composed of three, four, five, six, seven, eight, or more. The only requirement is that they stay within the bounds of the line-out dimensions. Remember, the side passing the ball in creates the length of the line-out.

The short line-out is used to introduce effective variety. In the three-man line-out, for example, the ball can be passed directly to a jumper or over the head of the last man. The last player can either race back and take the ball on the run, looking to the inside, or let it go over, bounce, and then pick it up.

Many times a side will not have any good jumpers, or the opposition has much better jumpers. To play an orthodox line-out, in this case, is essentially to give them the ball. The way to deal with it is to use a short line-out to neutralize their superiority. Just because everybody uses a full line-out doesn't mean it's gospel. A good side will adapt.

Remember, the ball can be thrown a long way out to the backline, but the pass must be straight, that is, coincide with the gain line. This tactic opens up the game and exploits a natural American talent—throwing the long spiral pass.

The Long Pass

In the line-out, the ball does not have to be thrown to a forward. The ball can be thrown long and directly out to a backline player. On your throw-in, and near your goal, is a dangerous situation. To get out of it, two plays can be used. The first is more orthodox. Throw the ball to number 4 (the center player in the line-out) because of the maximum amount of support and binding available on each side. A more exciting, and perhaps a more effective play, is to pass long directly to the flyhalf or inside center. As you can picture, in such an alignment, your backline is positioned flat against the gain line. The tackle line has advanced well toward the opposition side's backline. This means that its backs have to run farther to meet yours. The flyhalf or inside center can easily take the ball on the run, catching it directly on the gain line, and quickly kick for touch deep to the open side of the field. It really works.

The Passer

The player throwing the ball in, normally the hooker, has more to do than just pass. If your side wins the throw-in, then the passer must reinforce and come into the line-out and support. Usually, this will be at the front of the line-out if the ball has been thrown to two or four. Sometimes the jumper may have taken the ball down, but the opposition has somehow blocked the jumper from passing the ball back to the scrumhalf. The passer must then react and maul on the jumper, take the ball out, and pass it to the scrumhalf. If the ball is forced down by the jumper and a ruck forms, support must be directly to the ruck.

If, on the other hand, the throw results in the opposition winning the ball, responsibility is to protect the blind side or the ally. Whatever happens, never get caught or tied up in the line-out when playing defensively. Cover the ally and aim for the opposition scrumhalf when the ball is released.

6
FUNDAMENTALS OF BACKLINE PLAY

There are seven backline or backfield players: the scrumhalf (number 9), the flyhalf or outside half (number 10), the inside center (number 11), the outside center (number 12), the two wings (numbers 13 and 14), and the fullback (number 15).

Just as the forwards work as a unit and have objectives, so, too, the backline. The two basic objectives of the backline are:

1. Penetrate the gain line.
2. Stay in front of your forwards.

While playing rugby is for enjoyment, not everybody is cut out to play in the backline. New players to the game who are not perceived as forward material are usually shoved on the wing so that any damage they may do is kept at a minimum. Obviously, there has to be some kind of guideline to judge whether a player can be effective in the backline or not. The general rule is that to be an effective backline player one must be able to beat another backline player one-on-one—not every time, of course, but, given that chance, the potential back must have the speed, quickness, faking ability and/or power to make the break. If the player has a majority of these traits, then the ball handling and other basics can be learned. If the player has these traits but does not like to tackle or does not like contact, then it would be better to play another sport. This game should be played for fun and not to prove virility. Not everyone is cut out to be a rugby player.

But if rugby's the game, then it's very important to have good players as backs. In the backline a weak player will stand out like a chocolate stain on a white suit. In the forwards, it's not so obvious.

Factors in Backline Attack

In backline play two principles must be observed. On attack, the backline is always set deep from the gain line. As the ball moves out along the backline in this alignment, the players are

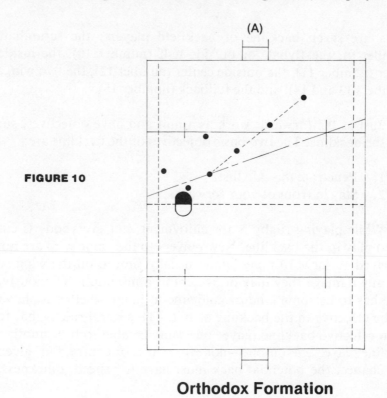

(A)

FIGURE 10

Orthodox Formation

running into open space and not into tacklers. The tackle line (refer to chapter 2, Gain Line and Tackle Line) will usually fall in the attacking side's half. The secret to alignment is to form up so that the tackle line is as coincident as possible with the gain line, and far enough forward to allow running room.

There are a few ways to align or form a backline. The first (see fig. 10(A)) is the orthodox backline where the players key on the scrumhalf, and all angle deep and on a straight line. The second (see fig. 10(B)) attacking alignment calls for a flatter formation. The backs are now keying on the flyhalf who has moved a bit deeper but the backline rotates forward toward the gain line. In this formation the tackle line has moved forward, yet the flyhalf and inside center still have plenty of room. The third (see fig. 10 (C)) formation is a new twist—a "W." The flyhalf starts deep as in the second formation. But the inside center now moves to an even deeper position. The outside center moves up and is on a line with the flyhalf. The wing aligns with or forward of the inside center.

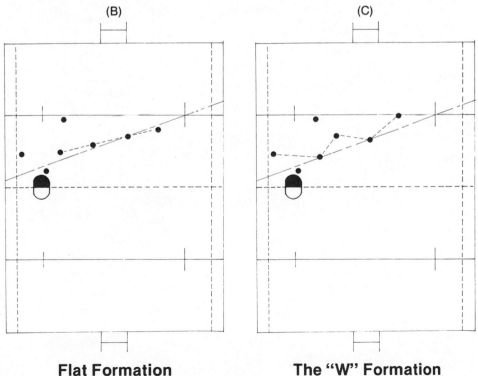

(B) (C)

Flat Formation   **The "W" Formation**

Here the flyhalf and the inside center have ample room to maneuver—they are running into plenty of open space and have a minimum of pressure. At the same time the tackle line is forward enough to cut down the distance the rest of the backline has to run to cross the gain line. This formation can still stretch the defense. The forward and aft positioning of backs can force the defense to break its straight line approach when moving up in a defensive alignment. Since the defensive player tries to keep his opposite to the outside and force play to the outside as well as move in close to tackle, the stagger of the attacking backs forces the defensemen to stagger in order to position themselves accordingly. A staggered defense often leaves gaps for the attack.

The key to effective backline attack revolves around three factors:

1. possession of the ball;
2. position on the field;
3. pace of the game—running, passing, and reacting.

FIGURE 11

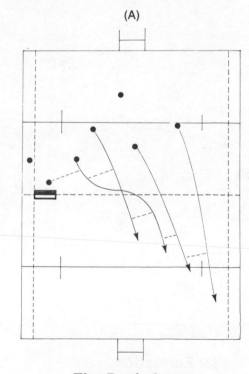

The Basic Loop

Without the ball, there is no attack. But even with possession, certain field moves work better than others. It depends on field position and play position. The following are just basic guidelines, not gospel.

After possession in the line-out, only outside moves should be used in the backline. The logic is simple. The forwards are all standing and in a better position to cover quickly. Keeping the ball moving out is safer, wiser, and usually more effective. As seen in Figure 11 (A–E), the basic four moves or plays to the outside are:

1. the outside loop to create the overlap;
2. the miss-one pass;
3. the extra man;
4. the quick ball.

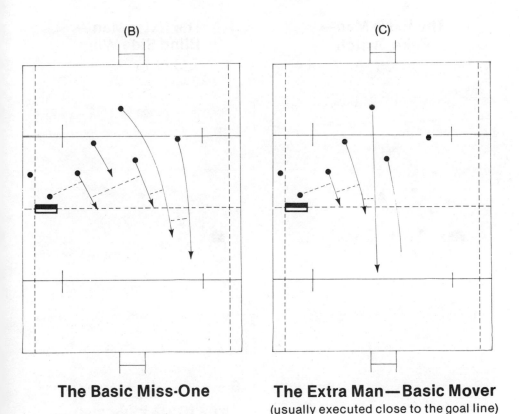

The Basic Miss-One

The Extra Man—Basic Mover
(usually executed close to the goal line)

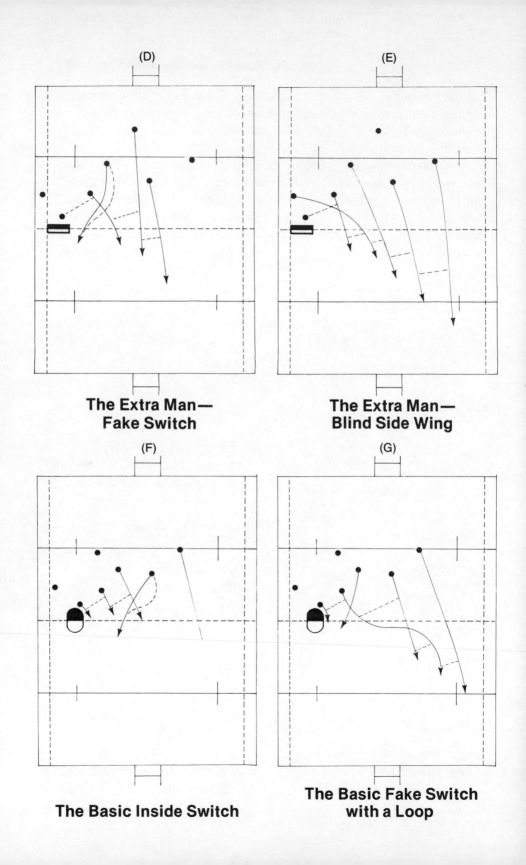

(D)

**The Extra Man—
Fake Switch**

(E)

**The Extra Man—
Blind Side Wing**

(F)

The Basic Inside Switch

(G)

**The Basic Fake Switch
with a Loop**

In the set scrum situation, the same four outside moves can be used, but, in addition, the following three inside moves can be added (see fig. 11(F-J)).

1. the inside switch to create a counter;
2. the attack to the blind side;
3. the extra man close to the goal line.

In ruck and maul situations, get the ball out fast. Rucks and mauls should never be prolonged. They are only momentary pauses in the flow of action. Since the activity around a ruck or a maul is never quite as predictable as a scrummage or line-out, it's better to get the ball out cleanly and then play-make. Otherwise, only use preplanned plays from the set pieces and penalty situations.

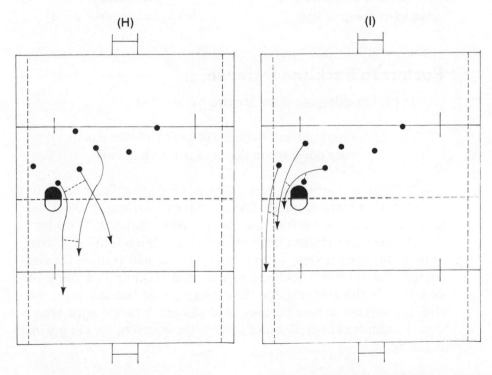

(H)

(I)

Switch to Inside Center   **Basic Attack to the Blind Side**

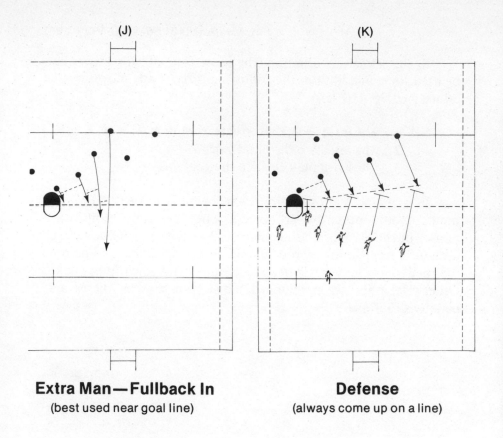

(J)　　　　　　　　　　　　**(K)**

Extra Man—Fullback In
(best used near goal line)

Defense
(always come up on a line)

Factors in Backline Defense

In backline defense there are two basic rules:

1. keep constant pressure to limit ball movement.
2. keep coverage in depth to get the ball back.

Without a doubt, the best defense is a good offense. And in this case it's a state of mind. The objective of defense is to get the ball back. And every effort must be geared to that end. Hard tackling is one way to intimidate the opposition, but it is not effective without the proper state of mind. Think: the ball is mine for the taking. To watch a backline execute solid tackling is a thing of beauty. It's sheer horror for the attacking side because it knows that the defense means business and will crash tackle with abandon. Establish your credentials early in the match by tackling with meaning.

On the other hand, there are basic guidelines. You just can't go up like a reckless headhunter.

The first thing is to move up on a line (see fig. 11(K)), especially the flyhalf and the two centers. Never move up faster or slower than your teammate, particularly the player inside you. If such a move occurs, the result is a staggered defensive alignment with the potential for gaps.

The second guideline is to keep inside your opposite to limit his options and force him to the sidelines. The objective is to flatten the attack by forcing play to the outside and stop any move to the inside. Obviously, as you approach the tackle you must be sure that you can react to a quick inside move. If your opposite is very fast, your inside position must be wider and more forward. Once a fast player turns the corner on you, it may be all over. But always turn and pursue. If, on the other hand, an inside move is successfully employed against you, turn and go with the player. Don't give up. Tackle from behind. Remember, your forwards are filling and covering from the inside and across the field.

Generally, in backline defense the rule of thumb is to play the ball, not the man, but don't go for interceptions. You must be able to "read" the man and still "cover" or "play" the ball. One method of doing this is to adopt a semizone defense whereby responsibility is with the flow of the ball. When switches or loops occur, the player in that zone always takes the ball. Why is it a semizone and not a full zone? Because with overlaps and other moves, one zone is essentially flooded, and the defensive player in the zone from where the ball came must react into the other zone to support. The zone is used as a frame of mind, not as a rigid rule. It's still "play" the ball and "read" the man.

In addition to the center of the backline, the wings and fullback constitute another aspect of defense. Their responsibility is for deep coverage against the run and the kick. The deep kick is usually taken by the fullback, but it will depend on the point to where the ball was kicked. Often the wing is in a better position to field the kick and initiate a counterattacking play with the fullback.

The wings and fullback do not come up and commit like the centers and flyhalf on defense. They must wait and react. The fullback must play defense like a deep safety (but only when his side does not have the ball). The wings must adopt a defense posture like outside safeties—back for the long ball and up fast for the run.

The Backline Positions

Scrumhalf. The scrumhalf is somewhat analogous to the quarterback in football. If you recall, when Walter Camp successfully had the rugby laws modified to become football rules, one of the crucial and most important changes was the possession rule. Possession was now to be guaranteed for three, then eventually four, plays of the ball. Since possession was assured, there was no reason for the scrumhalf to put the ball into the scrum. His responsibility now was to get the ball back from the hooker, who was in the center of the scrum. It was snapped back with the hooker's foot on a predetermined signal from the scrumhalf. And since the scrumhalf was positioned behind the line of forwards and halfway to the halfback, his title was changed to the quarterback. Now, back to rugby.

Again, the scrumhalf is the link. He or she essentially connects the forwards with the backline. The scrumhalf is also the pivot upon which all play starts. Probably the two most crucial responsibilities of the scrumhalf are passing the ball out to the backline (the service) and putting the ball into the scrum (the put-in).

In chapter 2 the basic spin pass was outlined, but since it is an important element, it will be reviewed. With the straight-out spin pass, the back foot is near the ball as it is scooped up (see fig. 12 (A) and (B)). The front foot is pointed in the direction of the pass.

FIGURE 12

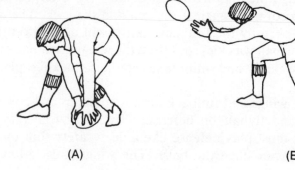

(A) (B)

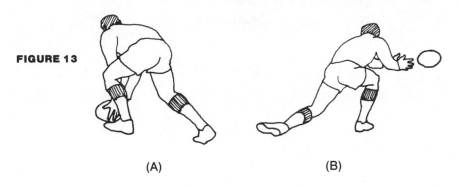

FIGURE 13

(A)   (B)

The action is a sweeping motion out. Power is generated by driving off the rear leg.

The scrumhalf must also be able to deliver a pivot pass. It is impossible always to deliver straight-out spin passes in a match. This is true on a put-in and a ball out of channel two. In this case the feet should be positioned so that the front foot is near the ball (see fig. 13 (A) and (B)). The scrumhalf can then pick up the ball, pivot on the ball of this foot, turn toward the direction of service, and simultaneously drive off and release the ball. Again the delivery of the pass should be waist high and force the flyhalf to reach for the ball on the run.

The second most critical responsibility of the scrumhalf is the put-in. The law states that the scrumhalf must stand one meter from the scrum, midway between the two front rows, holding the ball with both hands between the ankles and knees. The ball must be put-in quickly, directly and on a straight line with one single forward motion. No fakes allowed. The ball must hit the ground directly under the nearer prop's shoulder. No bounces either.

Putting the ball in has to be practiced. There are three ways to do it. The first (see fig. 14 (A)) is with the point turned into the tunnel. The second (see fig. 14 (B)) is with the side turned toward the scrum. And the third (see fig. 14 (C)) is with the point turned halfway toward the scrum.

The first way lacks control and should never be used because the hooker will strike the point of the ball and kick it out of the scrum. The second way is better but still presents a narrow target for the hooker's strike. This leaves the third way: the ball coming in on an angle. The key here is to hold the ball at the same angle as

FIGURE 14

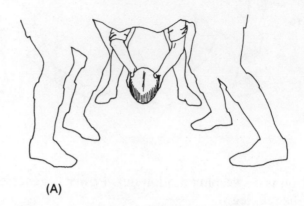

(A)

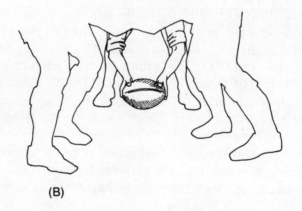

(B)

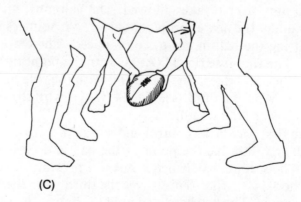

(C)

the hooker's striking foot so foot and ball meet nicely. The timing and speed of put-in are very important and must be practiced repeatedly between the front row and scrumhalf. Another thing to consider is that even though "no bounces," putting the ball in with a "slide" toward your hooker's foot is a good move. But if it's done too obviously, the scrumhalf will be called for "feeding," which is illegal.

Tactical kicking is also a part of scrumhalf play. In general, the two most effective kicks are the high punt for the up-and-under either to midfield or to the box (the area behind the opposition scrum or line-out and close to the near touch line), and the short grubber kick ahead. This kick is low and usually bounces several times.

The Flyhalf. As the scrumhalf is the pivot of the team and the link between backs and forwards, so the flyhalf is the pivot of the backline. This player is essentially the playmaker and sets the mood and pattern of attack. The flyhalf is the next player out from the scrumhalf on the backline and as a general rule, the deeper he is from the gain line, the farther out on the backline will any penetration occur. The flyhalf must never move off the mark until the scrumhalf has the ball in hand. Then he sets the pace of attack. If the flyhalf is off to a slower start, then the scrumhalf must quickly read this and deliver a slower ball.

At this position, good hands are a must. Every move depends on his catching the ball. No truer for anyone is the statement "if he can touch it, he can catch it" than it is for the flyhalf. While it is the responsibility of the scrumhalf to deliver good service, the flyhalf must have the ability to catch anything that comes into his area.

Angle of attack is also important for the flyhalf. Generally he should aim at the outside shoulder of the opposition flyhalf. A wider or flatter angle of attack will only force your own centers to go wider, move into each other, and limit the running room.

Passing quickly and accurately is another basic skill that is a must for a flyhalf. Just as running sets the pace or speed of the attack, so does passing. Slow passing slows up the backline, and fast passing speeds it up. Whatever, the flyhalf must never get caught flat footed because this will retard the whole backline movement.

46

The scrumhalf on attack. Here the scrumhalf has taken the ball from the scrum and is moving directly at the oposition wing forward (number 7). By forcing the wing forward to take on the scrumhalf, the flyhalf (partly behind the goal post) has room to maneuver, as does number 8 (the player standing and looking on). In this situation, both number 8 and the flyhalf are keying on the scrumhalf and will move to the open space.

Kicking is another important trait of the flyhalf. He should be able to do it with both feet. While this is the ideal, it is doubtful whether such players will come along all the time here. America is not a foot-oriented sports nation. Americans either throw a ball or run with it. If you give a ball to a child, it is unlikely he will kick it, even with the soccer boom here. The flyhalf must kick tactically and only to gain advantage. Otherwise, kicking is just giving up the ball. Nothing is more disheartening than a flyhalf who kicks aimlessly—and away from his forwards. It is usually a sign of not knowing what to do.

The two types of kicks most used out of this position are the short grubber kick ahead, usually done against a hard-hitting defense or a flat defensive alignment, and the punt. The punt can be a high hanger for an up-and-under to midfield or to the box. The other punt is the spiral to the touch line where, hopefully, the ball bounces before going out.

Obviously the flyhalf is important in defense. Many times flyhalves think that defense is not their game and that the back row of the forwards will take the opposite flyhalf. Nothing could be further from the truth. The flyhalf must take his opposite directly. The back row is there for support. The objective is to force the opposite flyhalf wide, or force him to go inside where you want him to go, and meet your wing forward. A tough-tackling flyhalf is a valuable weapon because it puts tremendous pressure on the other flyhalf.

Flyhalves can be any size, shape, or form as long as they can run, kick, pass, and tackle like champs. Most flyhalves seem to be mercurial players. But it is interesting to note what effect the performance of a very big player in this position would have. Such a player could take on the opposite flyhalf almost every play, forcing the flyhalf to commit to him and tackle. After this continual pressure on the opposite flyhalf, the defending back row must adapt and try to support its flyhalf, especially if the attacking flyhalf has run over the defending flyhalf a few times for long yardage and good field position. This is when a fast backline movement can be made with the ball. Up to this point the defense is not playing "honest" by stacking to stop the flyhalf's direct attack.

The Center Combination. Actually, the centers should not be isolated. What is important is the linkage between flyhalf and centers. These three players really work as one unit, both in attack and in defense.

The basic objective of this combination in attack is to stretch the defense out, especially the opposition centers. Stretching the defense means to force it to cover more and more ground away from its support. Obviously, if the stretch is too much—too wide across the field, the gain line will never be crossed and the backline men will start to crowd each other and limit running room. The rule is that when you catch yourself moving too wide across the field and too close to your other center or wing, turn straight upfield or quickly pass. Do not continue on the same course to the touch line.

The two centers have to know the basic skills thoroughly. They should be good ball handlers who run with abandon and tackle surely and hard. They should be able to "read" the man, "play" the ball, and always move up in a line when playing defense.

It used to be that on attack, the break at center was usually considered the "way to go." Today players on both sides are tough in these positions so sheer physical force is not always best. Therefore, more playmaking has to be incorporated. That's why the flyhalf is part of this combination. With three players working as a group it is easier to develop overlaps via switches and loops. It also puts much more pressure on the defense because with three players instead of two, it is now a more complex situation. The defense has more options to contend with before committing to a pressure point. It is precisely this hesitation that can help make the gap. Conversely, when playing defense the best move is all up on a line against the ball and tackling hard.

The Wing-Fullback Combination. The wing is usually the fastest man in the backline and sometimes the best broken-field ballcarrier. So get the ball to him. But get it to him at the right time! It is critical that the center combination works with the wing so that the ball gets there while the wing has room to run free from the other wing.

The wing must also work with the fullback in two very important ways. The first way is to bring the fullback into the line as an extra man. When this occurs the wing, as well as the centers, must be aware of the move and play accordingly in order to give room for him. It is folly to have the fullback come into the line only to be crowded out and have both players covered by one defensive player. In any event, the fullback into the line causes an extra man for the defense. Similarly, it also leaves the attacking side with no deep coverage. The weak side wing must therefore supply the deep coverage and rotate back into the fullback's area as the fullback goes forward and into the line for attack. If this rotation does not develop and the fullback gets tied up in a tackle, ruck, or maul, the attack has not only been neutralized, but a gigantic hole now exists behind the backline. If the opposition wins possession, and kicks ahead to take advantage of this situation (which they should), it's off to the scoring races.

Probably the one law change that affected fullback play more than any other was the change in the kick-for-touch law. Previously the fullback could roam very deep, never worry about coming into the line because kicking was his raison d'être. The fullback could stay back, swallow up deep kicks, and then from any point on the field boom the ball to touch. Today the law is that for a direct kick-to-touch (going out on the fly), the kicker must be behind the twenty-two-meter line.

So as play moves up the field and the fullback follows to support, kicking directly to touch was very difficult and sometimes impossible. To be good a kick had to go out on a bounce. The fullback now had to do more than kick. Cover defense and the extra man all became part of his responsibilities.

Besides deep cover defense and the extra man, another important wing-fullback relationship is the counterattack. Basically, in a counterattacking situation, the opposition while attacking presented the ball—a direct kick to your fullback or wing in a deep position—so that an attack could be mounted. Instead of engaging in a kicking contest, counterattacking is another move. The player taking the kick can retreat a bit and then race across field and initiate a reverse (or a fake reverse) with either the fullback (if the wing has caught the ball) or with the wing (if the fullback has caught the ball). The action is exactly like a reverse on a punt return where the two deep safeties cross and either reverse the ball or fake a reverse. Just remember, the player with the ball comes in front of the other player so as to shield the reverse or the fake. Both players should try to carry out the move as if each has the ball. This ploy will momentarily confuse the coverage and this hesitation may be all that is needed to find a gap to make a break.

Another counterattacking wing-fullback move is to "funnel" the defense. In covering a kick, the defense must spread out and blanket the field. The fullback or wing, after taking the kick, starts directly upfield. The ballcarrier essentially wants to have the defense key on this straight upfield move and "funnel" in. Simultaneously, the backline aligns as the defense converges. The ball then is quickly passed out to outflank the collapsing or funneling defense. Another aspect to this move is to use the long pass. As the defense collapses on the wing (or fullback) the ballcarrier stops and throws a long pass across to the open side of the field, hitting opposite wing. Most times this wing will not be covered. The "hold" (utilizing a reverse) and the "funnel" are two basic counterattacking moves. But to work, practice and communication are imperative. And to make practice worthwhile, a degree of coaching is essential. The next chapter will deal with this phase of the game.

7

Fundamentals of a Coaching Program

Coaching is a science as well as a profession. Over the last fifty years the U.S. has developed a coaching system for almost all sports in the high schools, colleges, and professional ranks. How to coach per se and how to organize are really not the problems in rugby. The problem is how you start. And this is what the last chapter will focus on.

Two major problems exist in coaching rugby. The first is philosophical. The second is more mundane and deals with knowledge and experience.

Basically, the philosophy behind playing rugby is that it's a player's game, not a coach's game. Most sports today are coach's games. The coach takes a dominant, if not *the* dominant, role in the team. This is especially true in schools and colleges and won't change. The coach says who will play and at what position. It is not a democracy. This is an established athletic tradition in this country.

The philosophy that rugby is a player's game is a carryover from the British, who never had coaching. Only in the last ten years or so was coaching on a scientific level introduced. Players in Britain, for example, grew up with rugby and learned the game through a combination of experience and osmosis. A coach was an afterthought. And most coaches, excluding physical education teachers, were usually either the captain or a retired player who devoted some time to the club. The selection of "who played what and where" was by committee. The coach had only one vote in the final selection.

In a short span of time, coaching rugby has taken on a more significant role overseas, because if a club or national side wants to have top representatives out on the field, they have to be well schooled; not only for that match, but beginning in grade school. A rugby coach, then, is important if a school, college, or club wants to develop a winning side. In fact, for rugby to succeed at all in the schools and colleges, coaching is the key. Good athletes gravitate toward a sport only when it is well organized and well coached. At that point it becomes popular and fun. In short, for high schools to start a rugby program, coaching is vital. For colleges to establish a rugby tradition, coaching is mandatory. And for clubs to attract graduates and sustain an enjoyable level of play, coaching is indispensable.

This by no means implies that the game must be handed over to coaches. On the contrary, to have everyone enjoy playing—from the first team to the third team—a coach is a valuable asset in maintaining stability. If you join a club as a member of the club, then no matter what side you play on, it's a function of how much time you're willing to give, the level of competition, and the coaching. That's the philosophical side of the problem. The second problem is more down to earth, and perhaps easier to solve. There just aren't enough rugby players who know how to organize a rugby coaching program. They know how to play the game. And they may know how to coach other sports. But they don't know how to start coaching rugby. However, it's a problem that can easily be solved.

The first major generation of rugby players—now in their mid-thirties or older—learned the game "on the job." The next and future generations of rugby players must learn the game from coaches as well as through experience. This means coaching through our own system and setting our own style of play. It is myopic at best, and ignorant at worst, to think that by importing coaches our problems will be solved. A coaching infrastructure must be built through established former players—no matter what level—who want to take the time to put something back into the game. And this includes the schools, because in the long run they will determine the future calibre of rugby in the United States.

It is, of course, the responsibility of the United States of America Rugby Football Union to formalize a coaching program and set up clinics around the country to train coaches. Hopefully, this book can serve as a guide to help players begin to coach. This last chapter focuses on how to set up some basic drills to improve individual player skills as well as team play, with the hope that it will make a practice session more enjoyable. From trying these drills coaching innovation must follow. This material should serve only as a foundation. With time, each coach should be able to improve, modify, change, or invent drills and practices to meet personnel and competition.

Physical education teachers and coaches of other school sports who are starting rugby understand the advantages and principles of organizing a good practice session. And with their experience, setting one up will not present too difficult a problem. The key element for any good practice session is *planning*. Sixty minutes of concentrated effort is worth more than two hours of just running around.

Basic Ball Handling Drill

Most clubs start practice by passing the ball. The problem is that too often passing is done in a haphazard manner and ends up more as an exercise or warmup rather than skill improvement. Force a bit of concentration on passing. Put a little pressure into the drill so that players must concentrate and pass the ball correctly.

The best way to establish artificial pressure is to set up a series of grids each ten meters square with a flag or marker at the corners. All passing must occur within this grid system (see fig. 15).

For example, starting with three lines of players, the first three players move down the grids (three grids) passing the ball.

FIGURE 15

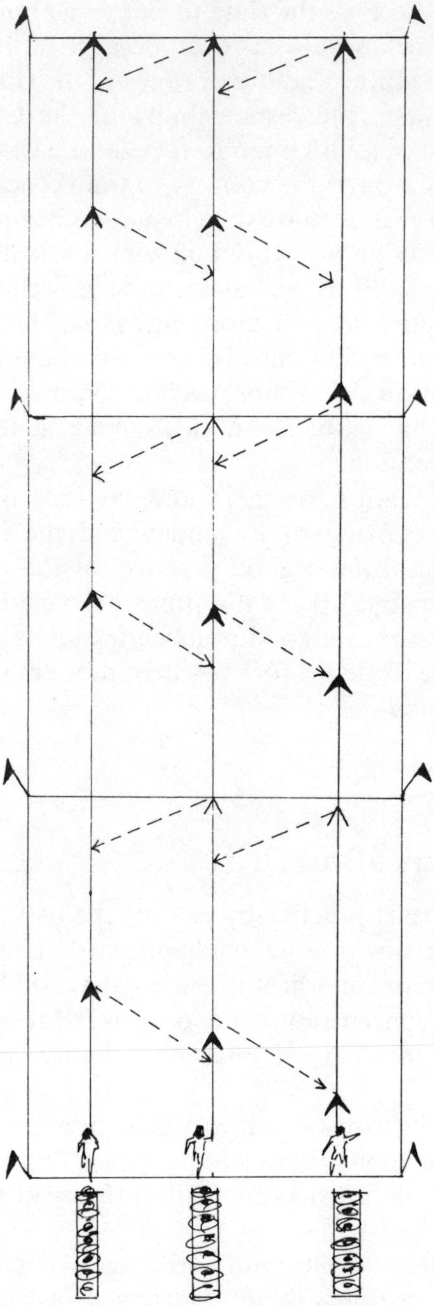

The grid forces them to align properly and to pass correctly. From this setup, four types of passes should be practiced.

1. the basic swing pass at normal delivery;
2. the basic swing pass delivered from below the knees;
3. a high pass delivered from above the head;
4. the quick pass (a rapid catch-pass move).

Each player should go through this series of passes from each of the three positions within the grid.

There are variations to this drill. For one, a fourth player could be added for close passing. And moves such as the loop, with the outside player looping the others and then back, could be added. Even switches could be incorporated. Each player should never return to the same line. They should have a crack at each position in the grid: outside, middle, and inside.

Basic Passing and Alignment Drill for Backs

This drill is designed to force backs to both pass the ball quickly and to align even quicker (see fig. 16). The drill is simple, but needs a good many balls. A full backline is set up. There are four balls spaced about twenty yards apart. As the flyhalf moves forward the first pass is delivered and he passes it out as quickly and as accurately as possible. He then races on, without stopping, to the next pass twenty yards ahead. The process is repeated for all four balls. In the initial stages the ball should end up with the wing, who then puts the ball down and sets up for the next pass. If a player drops a pass tell him to forget it and get ready for the next pass. But keep a record of who drops the most passes—and then find out why. As soon as the first backline is past the third ball, have another backline ready to go. Never keep players idle. The drill should be run at least six times per backline.

As the season progresses, the drill can be improved by adding moves into the backline. The coach can call out a switch or a loop or even an extra man by bringing the fullback into the drill. When adding these moves, the balls should be spaced farther apart.

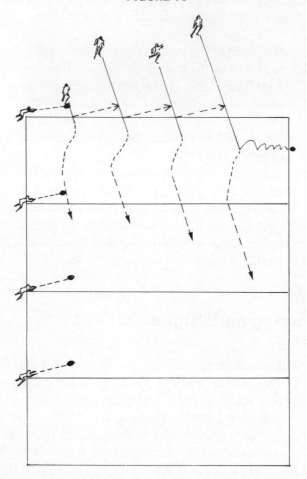

FIGURE 16

There could be two, three, or four backlines ready to do this drill, one right on the heels of the other. Think of it as almost running plays, just like gridiron football.

Basic Man on Man

The idea here is that the grid provides constraint and the opposition the pressure. One player on defense and two on attack (see fig. 17 (A)). The object of drill is practicing when to pass. As the defending player moves into the ballcarrier, the ballcarrier

FIGURE 17

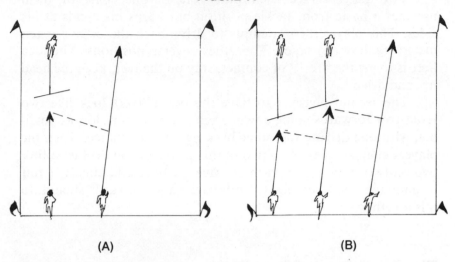

(A)   (B)

must pass out at a point where pressure on him is almost at a maximum—the point where the defender has committed.

The three-on-two is more complex but also a very good drill (see fig. 17 (B)). Three players are on attack and two on defense. The player with the ball must make the first defender commit to him. The key is to pass at that point where the middle player has the least amount of pressure facing him even though there is a second defender. If the pass is made too soon, the first defender can cover the middle player, leaving room for the second defender to cover the third player. If the pass is made too late, then the middle player will be trapped because defender and ball arrived at the same time.

Modification to the drill can include a quick pass back to one from two, a loop, or even a switch. The purpose of the drill is really twofold—passing and defending. It is a real pressure situation drill.

Basic Contact Drill

Since rugby is a contact sport, confidence in body contact is vital to good tackling, rucking, mauling, and scrummaging. By starting off with the following drill, confidence is developed.

Two players face each other one-on-one. One of them assumes a basic front tackle position but keeps his hands at his sides. This player then attempts to drive back the other for ten meters against resistance. Then they reverse positions. The idea here is to get the "feel" of contact, stay on the feet, keep the head up, and drive.

The second phase is to have the two players lock like two front-row forwards going down. Each player goes as low as possible, with one driving the other back against resistance. Then the players change roles. Step two in this phase of the drill is to link two-on-two, then three-on-three, five-on-five, and finally a full scrummage—eight-on-eight. Both backs and forwards should do this together.

The Basic Ruck/Maul Drill

This drill also uses the grids (see fig. 18 (A)). Four players start at point A and ruck at 1. The last player to the ruck becomes the scrumhalf. At the coach's whistle the players disengage from the ruck and ruck at 2. The player who was at the scrumhalf position at 1 is the first into the ruck at 2. The procedure continues. The resistance at 1, 2, 3, and 4 are two players who are bound together with their backs facing the oncoming four players.

The maul drill is essentially the same except that the ball is out in front of one resistance player (see fig. 18 (B)). The first player to the ball picks it up and drives into this resistance. The other two players maul and the fourth plays scrumhalf. This fourth player could also maul. After the whistle the four disengage and sprint to the next maul. Remember also, both drills can be done with more than four players. Another modification is to have the rucking or mauling players start either on their knees or on their backs. Again, backs and forwards should do this drill jointly.

Basic Tackling Drill

The grids are used again, except this time the grid could be reduced to five yards in depth. Three tacklers are on their backs,

FIGURE 18

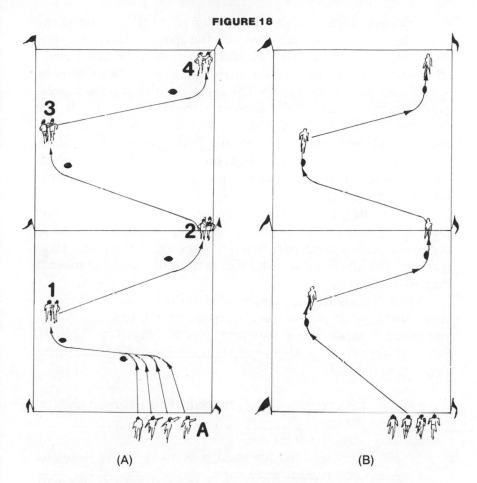

(A)   (B)

each with a number. There is one ballcarrier. When the coach calls out a number, that player gets up and moves to tackle. The ball-carrier can vary his path, thereby making the tacklers all practice front and side tackles. The important point to remember is that this is a drill, not competition. Let the tackle occur.

Unopposed and Semi-opposed

Sometimes this is called shadow rugby. Unopposed means basically running plays up and down the field. The difference here is that football is stop-and-go, while rugby is continuous. But the theory is the same. Repetition builds reaction to situations.

Unopposed starts with fifteen players on the field and the coach dictating continuous moves on the spot. Normally it starts with a scrum at the 22. As the ball moves out, the coach gives commands for what is to be done. He may call a ruck or maul or the fullback-in or even a loop. The coach dictates and the players must respond. Even penalty situations should be practiced. The drill should go up the field nonstop, turn, and start down with a line-out and then repeat back up the field. The key is not how many times a side goes up and back, but how many times it can do it in five or ten minutes. The coach must set the time and be on the field running with the players.

The second part is to add some opposition pressure. It is only there for practicing proper scrummaging, line-outs, and field alignment. This second part is still unopposed in that there is no tackling. The attacking side still moves the ball according to what the coach calls out.

The unopposed and semi-opposed are designed to develop a sense of the game and to force everyone to link together. When you practice, stress those four principles of play: Go Forward, Support, Keep the Ball Alive, and Maintain Pressure. Some of the elements to remember are:

1.   Let everyone handle the ball. This lets everyone feel a part of the team.
2.   Vary the situations.
3.   Realize when the team is breaking down—making too many errors. Stop and review.
4.   Use a whistle.

The Kickoff

The final aspect of team play is the kickoff and the reception. Most clubs take these, as well as dropouts, for granted (see fig. 19). Basically, the kickoff should be to your advantage, not theirs. If your side does not have big forwards or a good jumper who can get down on the ball and snare it in the air, then why kick to their forwards? Kick the ball away from their strength. Kick the ball deep or kick it to the open side of the field. There's no rule that says you must kick it to the forwards on kickoffs. It is amazing

FIGURE 19

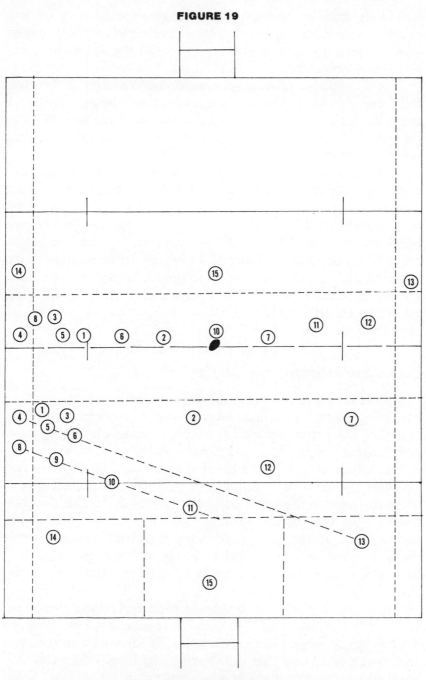

The Kickoff

how many clubs put the ball right into the opposition's pack and give it a great platform attack. Never, never kick the ball to their forwards unless your forwards can either get the ball on the kick-off, or overpower the opposition.

On a dropout it is the exact same thing. Why kick to their forward strength twenty-five or more meters from the goal line? Kick the ball deep and away. Have your side race to the ball. Even go for touch way upfield if you have a kicker who can get it out on a good bounce.

On receiving a kickoff three zones must be covered, the forward zone, the open-side zone, and the deep zone. As you can see from Figure 19 the three deep players (13, 14, and 15) can manage the deep zone fairly well. They can also come into the line on a backline movement if needed. Numbers 2, 12, and 7 have the open-side zone responsibility. And the forwards speak for themselves. Notice also that if a kick is to the forwards, the backline is already formed, starting with the scrumhalf (9), the flyhalf (10), and the inside center (11).

Basic Scrummaging Drills

Most important to remember is that scrummaging is a vital part of the game, and it must be practiced. If you recall, there are over forty set scrums per match, so practicing scrummaging is not only necessary to develop good technique, but also fitness.

The following drill is a good starting one. First set up two packs of forwards in a scrumdown position. The coach should make sure that in this setup stage all the players lean against one another—no shoving or pushing. Look at each position. Make comments regarding each player's leg, hip, back, and arm positioning. Crawl into the tunnel and look at the position of their feet. Make necessary adjustments if they are straining in the wrong way.

Next, start with one side snap-shoving against the other for a series of five or six times. Then do the reverse. Do not introduce the ball in this second stage. After you are satisfied that the positioning is correct and that the shove is right, introduce the ball. First start with no competition, i.e., automatic possession. Again repeat this until both sides have started to master the snap-shove and drive coupled with the sweep of the ball by the hooker. Repeat this at least twenty times for each side.

Now apply pressure—competition for the ball. Both hookers should go for the ball. Use your scrumhalf in this phase. Have him put the ball in. Both packs should practice this until you feel comfortable with the progress. Do not prolong it because as both packs tire, and bad habits will creep in.

The final stage is to add both pressure and fitness. Set up both scrums and introduce the ball competitively. Make one side, designated previously, break from the scrum, run ten or fifteen yards to a marker, and then run back to scrumdown. Put the ball in competitively using your scrumhalf. Repeat this several times with one side, then reverse it. Subsequently, adding both distance and repetition will increase both technique and fitness if done under control.

Basic Line-Out Drills

The line-out is not an afterthought. In fact, it is a more effective platform from which to mount an attack since everyone is up and in a better position to go forward.

Practice in the line-out must incorporate the principles of what constitutes winning a line-out. These are:

1. An accurate pass.
2. Proper timing between jumper and passer.
3. Tight binding and support (forming that wall).
4. Everyone knowing the signals.
5. Everyone knowing his job.

The drill procedures are quite simple. First set up a line-out and have a review. Then start with unopposed passing to each of the jumpers (tap and take-downs). Move to the peel both front and back.

After you are satisfied, add pressure. Introduce competition at the jumper positions, then a full line-out. Finally, add maximum pressure by having two complete line-outs. But don't stop there. After each line-out have both teams sprint to another position along the touchline and start a new line-out. Repeat this until break-downs occur. Then always repeat the fundamentals.

Basic Statistics

In order for a coach to evaluate a team's or player's performance properly, an objective look at what's happening on the field is vital. Proper statistics help that evaluation.

There are basically four aspects of play that should be measured—the set scrums, the line-outs, the rucks/mauls, and the penalties. In the first, the statistics should show how many times possession was obtained on your ball-in and how many times on their ball your scrum took possession. The same is true for line-outs—how often possession was obtained on your throw-in and how often on theirs.

The loose ball is another key indicator. Here both rucks and mauls could be combined to see how often total loose ball was won. This is important because it will indicate how fast and how aggressively your team is moving after the ball.

The final statistics, penalties, are useful to determine who knows the rules, so a review of the laws infringed can be conducted at the next practice and guard against repetition. Penalties can kill a team's momentum.

Appendix:

U.S.A.R.F.U. LAWS OF RUGBY FOOTBALL 1977-78

Object of the Game

The object of the game is that two teams of fifteen players each, observing fair play according to the laws and a sporting spirit should, by carrying, passing, and kicking the ball, score as many points as possible, the team scoring the greater number of points to be the winner of the match.

Declaration of Amateurism

The game is an amateur game. No one is allowed to seek or to receive payment or other material reward for taking part in the game.

Definitions

The following terms have the meaning assigned to them:

Beyond or *Behind* or *In front* of any position implies "with both feet," except when unsuited to the context.

Dead means that the ball is for the time being out of play. This occurs when the referee blows his whistle to indicate a stoppage of play or when an attempt to convert a try is unsuccessful.

Defending Team means the team in whose half of the ground the stoppage of play occurs and the opponents of the defending team are referred to as *"the Attacking Team."*

Kick. A kick is made by propelling the ball with any part of the leg or foot (except the heel), from knee to toe inclusive. If the player is holding the ball, he must propel it out of his hands, or if it is on the ground, he must propel it a visible distance.

Drop Kick. A drop kick is made by letting the ball fall from the hand (or hands) to the ground and kicking it at the first rebound as it rises.

Place Kick. A place kick is made by kicking the ball after it has been placed on the ground for that purpose.

Punt. A punt is made by letting the ball fall from the hand (or hands) and kicking it before it touches the ground.

Mark. The mark is the place at which a free kick or penalty kick is awarded.

Line Through the Mark (or Place). Except where specifically stated otherwise, the words "a line through the mark" or "a line through the place" always means a line parallel to the touch line.

Union means the controlling body under whose jurisdiction the match is played and in the case of an International Match it means the International Rugby Football Board or a Committee thereof.

Other definitions are included in and have effect as part of the laws.

Laws

Law 1. Ground.

The field-of-play is the area as shown on the plan, bounded by, but not including, the goal lines and touch lines.

The playing enclosure is the field-of-play, In-goal and a reasonable area surrounding them.

The *Plan*, including all words and figures thereon, is to take effect as part of these Laws.

The *Terms* appearing on the Plan are to bear their apparent meaning and to be deemed part of the definition as if separately included.

(1) All lines shown on the plan must be suitably marked out. The touch lines are in touch. The goal lines are In-goal. The dead-ball line is *not*

in In-goal. The touch-in-goal lines and corner posts are in touch-in-goal. The goal posts are to be erected in the goal lines.

(2) The game must be played on a ground of the area (maximum) shown on the plan and marked in accordance with the plan. The surface must be grass-covered or, where this is not available, clay or sand provided the surface is not of dangerous hardness.

(3) Any objection by the visiting team about the ground or the way in which it is marked out must be made to the referee before the first kick-off.

Law 2. Ball.

(1) The ball when new shall be oval in shape of four panels and of the following dimensions:

Length in line. . . . . 280 to 300 mm
Circumference (end on) . . . . 760 to 790 mm
Circumference (in width) . . . . 580 to 620 mm
Weight. . . . . 400 to 440 gms

(2) The dimensions of the ball may be reduced only for younger schoolboys.

(3) Balls may be specially treated to make them resistant to mud and easier to grip. The casings need not be of leather.

NOTES:

Γ indicates post with flag.
Length and breadth of field to be as near to dimensions indicated as possible. All areas to be rectangular.

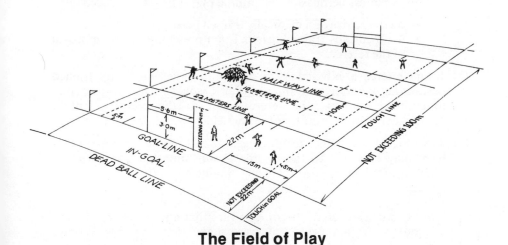

The Field of Play

— — — These broken lines indicate 10 meters distance from the halfway line and 5 meters distance from the touch lines.

— These lines at the goal lines and intersecting the 22 meters and 10 meters lines and the halfway line are 15 meters from the touch lines.

The lines at the goal lines extend 5 meters into the field of play.

Goal dimensions:—3 meters is taken the ground to the top edge of the crossbar, and 5.60 meters inside to inside of the goal posts.

Where practicable the intersection of the dead-ball line and touch-in-goal lines should be indicated by a flag. A minimum height of 1.20 meters above the ground is desirable for corner posts.

Law 3. Number of Players.

(1) A match shall be played by not more than fifteen players in each team.

(2) Replacement of players shall be allowed in recognized trial matches as determined by the Unions having jurisdiction over the match.

(3) In all other matches, a player may be replaced only on account of injury and subject to the following conditions:—

   a) Not more than two players in each team may be replaced.

   b) A player who has been replaced must NOT resume playing in the match.

(4) a) In matches in which a national representative team is playing, a player may be replaced ONLY when, in the opinion of a medical practitioner, the player is so injured that he should not continue playing in the match.

   b) For such competition and other domestic matches as a Union gives express permission, an injured player may be replaced—

   • on the advice of a medically trained person, or
   • if a medically trained person is not present, with the approval of the referee.

(5) If the referee is advised by a doctor or other medically trained person that a player is so injured that it would be harmful for him to continue playing, the referee shall, if the player's captain agrees, require the player to leave the field.

(6) Any objection by either team as regards the number of players in a team may be made to the referee at any time but the objection shall not affect any score previously obtained.

   NOTE

   i   As soon as a referee becomes aware that a team has more than the correct number of players on the field, he must require the captain of that team to reduce the number of players appropriately.

Law 4. Players' Dress.

(1) A player must not wear dangerous projections such as buckles or rings.

(2) Shoulder pads of the "harness" type must not be worn. If the referee is satisfied that a player requires protection following an injury to a shoulder, the wearing of a pad of cottonwool, sponge rubber or similar soft material may be permitted provided the pad is attached to the body or sewn on to the jersey.

(3) Studs of a player's boots must be of leather, rubber, aluminum or any approved plastic. They must be circular, securely fastened to the boots and of the following dimensions:

Length (maximum). 18mm
        (measured from sole)
Diameter at base (minimum). 13mm
Diameter at top (minimum) 10mm
Minimum diameter of washer 20mm
        (if separate from stud)

(4) The referee has power to decide before or during the match that any part of a player's dress is dangerous. He must then order the player to remove the dangerous part and permit him to resume playing in the match only after it has been removed.

Law 5. Toss, Time.

No-side is the end of a match.

(1) Before a match begins the captains shall toss for the right to kick-off or the choice of ends.

(2) The duration of play in a match shall be such time not exceeding eighty minutes as shall be directed by the Union or, in the absence of such directions, as agreed upon by the teams or, if not agreed, as fixed by the referee. In International matches two periods of forty minutes each shall be played.

NOTE

i   The term "not exceeding eighty minutes" excludes any extra time which the Union may direct or authorize to be played in the case of a drawn match in a knock-out competition.

(3) Play shall be divided into two halves. At halftime the teams shall change ends and there shall be an interval of not more than five minutes.

(4) A period not exceeding two minutes shall be allowed for any other permitted delay. A longer period may be allowed only if the additional time is required for the removal of an injured player from the field-of-play. Playing time lost as a result of any such permitted delay or of delay in taking a kick at goal shall be made up in the half of the match in which the delay occurred, subject to the power vested in the referee to declare no-side before time has expired.

NOTE

ii   The referee must make up time lost through any delay in taking a kick at goal. This applies whether or not the referee considers the delay to be "undue delay" on the part of the kicker. Playing time lost should begin from 40 seconds after the player has indicated his intention to kick at goal.

Law 6. Referee and Touch Judges.

A. Referee.

(1) There shall be a referee for every match. He shall be appointed by or under the authority of the Union or, in case no such authorized referee has been appointed, a referee may be mutually agreed upon between the teams or, failing such agreement, he shall be appointed by the home team.

(2) If the referee is unable to officiate for the whole period of a match a replacement shall be appointed either in such manner as may be directed by the Union, or in the absence of such direction, by the referee or, if he is unable to do so, by the home team.

(3) The referee shall keep the time and the score, and he must in every match apply fairly the Laws of the Game without any variation or omission, except only when the Union has authorized the application of an experimental law approved by the International Board.

NOTES

i   If the referee is in doubt as to the correct time he should consult either or both of the touch judges. Only if the information given by them is insufficient may he consult another person.

ii   Where the referee allows time for delays the time must be made up in the half of the match in which the delay occurs.

iii The referee has power to declare no-side before time has expired

if, in his opinion, the full time cannot for any reason be played
or continuance of play would be dangerous.

iv Where a player is injured, the referee should not alow more than
two minutes delay unless a longer period is necessary to remove
the player, or to give essential treatment on the field-of-play.

v The referee should not allow time for injury if he has reason to
believe that a player is feigning injury. In such circumstances he
should order the player to be removed immediately from the
field-of-play and then order play to be resumed forthwith.

vi The referee should, when the ball is dead, allow time for a player
to replace or repair a badly torn jersey or shorts. He must not allow time for a player to retie or repair a bootlace.

(4) He must not give any instruction or advice to either team prior to the
match. During the match he must not consult with anyone except
only

a) either or both touch judges on a point of fact relevant to their
functions, or

b) in regard to time.

(5) The referee is the sole judge of fact and of law. All his decisions are
binding on the players. When he has given a decision he cannot alter
it except only a decision given before he observes that the touch
judge's flag remains raised.

(6) The referee must carry a whistle and must blow it

a) to indicate the beginning of the match, half-time, resumption of
play after half time, no-side, a score or a touch-down and

b) to stop play because of infringement or otherwise as required by
the Laws.

NOTES

vii The referee has power to stop the match at any time by blowing
his whistle but he must not do so except on the occasions indicated in Law 6 Λ (6) which include the following:

a) when he orders a scrummage;
b) when the ball has touched or crossed the touch,
touch-in-goal, or dead-ball lines;
c) when the ball has been grounded in In-goal;
d) when the ball is unplayable in a ruck, maul or lineout;
e) when he stops for an offense under Law 26 (3) prior to
ordering off or cautioning the offender; and in such a case he
must whistle a second time when he awards the penalty try or
kick;

f) when he awards a penalty kick or free kick;

g) when he allows a fair-catch;

h) when the ball or a player carrying it has touched him and one team has therefrom gained an advantage;

i) when a player is injured but only when the ball next becomes dead unless (j) below applies;

j) when continuance of play would be dangerous.

viii The referee should whistle for halftime or no-side as soon as time has expired if the ball be dead or if the ball be in play when the time has expired, as soon as the ball next becomes dead.

If the ball becomes dead after time has expired

a) as the result of a try the referee shall allow the kick to be taken and then whistle for halftime or no-side, or if it be

b) as the result of a fair catch, free kick or penalty kick the referee shall allow play to proceed until the ball next becomes dead.

If time expires before the ball is put into a scrummage or is thrown in from touch, the referee must whistle for half time or no-side.

(7) During a match no person other than the players, the referee and the touch judges may be within the playing enclosure or the field-of-play unless with the permission of the referee which shall be given only for a special and temporary purpose.

NOTES

ix The referee should, when necessary, but not before he indicates his permission, allow baggage attendants and doctors or first aid personnel to enter the playing enclosure and field-of-play. He should be strict in refusing permission to persons intending to give advice or instructions to a team, and players should not be allowed to leave the field-of-play to get advice or instructions. Latitude should, however, be allowed in recognized trial matches.

x Apart from injury the referee should not allow a player to leave the playing enclosure except in special circumstances.
The referee should not permit a player to resume until the ball is dead.

xi The referee must not permit a team or individual players to leave the field-of- play in order to change jerseys.

xii If a player who has retired on account of injury or other reason resumes playing without the permission of the referee, the referee should impose penalties for misconduct if he considers that the offense was willful for the purpose of assisting his team or obstructing the opponents. If the offense was not willful interference and if the offending team gains an advantage the referee should order a scrummage at the place where the player resumed playing without permission, and the opposing team shall put in the ball.

(8) a) All players must respect the authority of the referee and they must not dispute his decisions. They must (except in the case of a kick-off) stop playing at once when the referee has blown his whistle.

b) A player must when so requested whether before or during the match, allow the referee to inspect his dress.

c) A player must not leave the playing enclosure without the referee's permission. If a player retires during a match because of injury or otherwise, he must not resume playing in that match until the referee has given him permission.

Penalty: Infringement by a player is subject to penalty as misconduct.

B. Touch Judges.

(1) There shall be two touch judges for every match. Unless touch judges have been appointed by or under the authority of the Union, it shall be the responsibility of each team to provide a touch judge.

(2) A touch judge is under the control of the referee who may instruct him as to his duties and may over-rule any of his decisions. The referee may request that an unsatisfactory touch judge be replaced and he has power to order off and report to the Union a touch judge who in his opinion is guilty of misconduct.

(3) Each touch judge shall carry a flag (or other suitable object) to signal his decisions. There shall be one touch judge on each side of the ground and he shall remain in touch except wen judging a kick at goal.

(4) He must hold up his flag when the ball or a player carrying it has gone into touch and must indicate the place of throw in and which team is entitled to do so. He must also signal to the referee when the ball or a player carrying it has gone into touch-in-goal.

(5) The touch judge shall lower his flag when the ball has been thrown in except on the following occasions when he must keep it raised:—

a) when the player throwing in the ball puts any part of either foot in the field-of-play,

b) when the ball has not been thrown in by the team entitled to do so.

It is for the referee to decide whether or not the ball has been thrown in from the correct place.

(6) When a kick at goal from a try or penalty kick is being taken both tough judges must assist the referee by signalling the result of the kick. One touch judge shall stand at or behind each of the goal posts and shall raise his flag if the ball goes over the cross bar.

Law 7. Mode of Play.

A match is started by a kick-off, after which any player who is on-side may at any time

- catch or pick up the ball and run with it,

- pass, throw or knock the ball to another player,

- kick or otherwise propel the ball,

- tackle, push or shoulder an opponent holding the ball,

- fall on the ball,

- take part in scrummage, ruck, maul or line-out,

    provided he does so in accordance with these Laws.

NOTE

i   If a player hands the ball to another player of his team without any propulsion or throwing of the ball, this does not constitute a pass.

Law 8. Advantage.

(1) The referee shall not wistle for an infringement during play which is followed by an advantage gained by the non-offending team. An advantage must be either territorial or such possession of the ball as constitutes an obvious tactical advantage. A mere opportunity to gain advantage is not sufficient.

(2) The only occasions when advantage does not apply are:—

- when, at a kick-off, the ball is not kicked from the correct place or by the correct form of kick,

- when the ball emerges from either end of the tunnel at a scrummage,

- when at a drop-out the kick is taken otherwise than by a drop kick,

- when a free-kick is void,

- when the ball or a player carrying it touches the referee.

NOTES

i   The referee is given a wide discretion as to what constitutes an advantage and is not limited to a territorial advantage. The referee is the sole judge of whether an advantage has been gained.

ii   The only occasions when advantage does not apply are those stated in (2) of this Law.

iii   When any irregularity of play not provided for in the Laws occurs, a scrummage shall be formed where the irregularity occurred. In deciding which team should put in the ball, the referee should apply Law 20 (7).

Law 9. Ball or Player Touching Referee.

(1) If the ball or a player carrying it touches the referee in the field-of-play, play shall continue unless the referee considers either team has gained an advantage in which case he shall order a scrummage. The team which last played the ball shall put it in.

(2) (a) If the ball in a player's possession or a player carrying it touches the referee in that player's In-goal, a touch-down shall be awarded.

      (b) If a player carrying the ball in his opponents' In-goal touches the referee before grounding the ball, a try shall be awarded at that place.

NOTES

i   If the ball, while in play in In-goal at either end but not held by a player, touches the referee, a touch judge, or a spectator, a touch-down shall be awarded provided that a touch-down would otherwise have been obtained or the ball would have gone into touch-in-goal or on or over the dead-ball line.

ii   If the ball while in play in In-goal at either end, but not held by a player, touches the referee, a touch judge, or a spectator, a try shall be awarded at that place provided an attacking player would otherwise have scored it.

iii   When the ball touches a spectator in either of the above cases, if the referee is in doubt, the award shall be made top the visiting team if that team is the defending team under (i) or the attacking team under (ii).

Law 10. Kick-Off.

Kick-off is (a) a place kick taken from the center of the halfway line by a team which has the right to start the match or by the opposing team on the resumption of play after the halftime interval or by the defending team after a goal has been scored, or (b) a drop kick taken at or from behind the center of the halfway line by the defending team after an unconverted try.

(1) The ball must be kicked from the correct place; otherwise it shall be kicked off again.

(2) The ball must reach the opponents' ten meters line, unless first played by an opponent; otherwise it shall be kicked off again, or a scrummage formed at the center, at the opponents' option. If it reaches the ten meters line and is then blown back, play shall continue.

(3) If the ball pitches directly into touch, touch-in-goal or over or on the dead-ball line, the opposing team may accept the kick, have the ball kicked off again, or have a scrummage formed at the center.

(4) The **kicker's team** must be behind the ball when kicked; otherwise a scrummage shall be formed at the center.

(5) The **opposing team** must stand on or behind the ten meters line. If they are in front of that line or if they charge before the ball has been kicked, it shall be kicked off again.

Law 11. Method of Scoring.

Try. A try is scored by first grounding the ball in the opponents' In-goal. A try may be awarded if one would probably have been scored but for obstruction, unfair play, foul play or misconduct by the opposing team.

Goal. A goal is scored by kicking the ball over the opponents' cross-bar and between the goal posts from the field-of-play by any place kick or drop kick, except a kick-off, drop-out or free kick, without touching the ground or any player of the kicker's team.
A goal is scored if the ball has crossed the bar, even though it may have been blown backwards afterwards, and whether it has touched the cross-bar or either goal post or not.
A goal is scored if the ball has crossed the bar notwithstanding a prior offense of the opposing team.
A goal may be awarded if the ball is illegally touched by any player of the opposing team and if the referee considers that a goal would otherwise probably have been scored.

The scoring values are as follows:—

A try. . . . . 4 points

A goal from a try (in which case the try
    shall not count) . . . . 6 points

A goal from a penalty kick . . . . 3 points

A dropped goal otherwise obtained. . . . . 3 points

Law 12. Try and Touch-Down.

Grounding the ball is the act of a player who

a) *while holding the ball in his hand (or hands) or arm (or arms) brings the ball in contact with the ground, or*

b) *while the ball is on the ground either*

- *places his hand (or hands) or arm (or arms) on it with downward pressure, or*

- *falls upon it and the ball is anywhere under the front of his body from waist to neck inclusive.*

Picking up the ball from the ground is not grounding it.

A. Try.

(1) A player who is on-side scores a try when

- he carries the ball into his opponents' In-goal, or

- the ball is in his opponents' In-goal, and he first grounds it there.

(2) The scoring of a try includes the following cases:—

a) If a player carries, passes, knocks or kicks the ball into his In-goal and an opponent first grounds it,

b) if, at a scrummage or ruck, a team is pushed over its goal line and before the ball has emerged it is first grounded in In-goal by an attacking player,

c) if the momentum of a player, when held in possession of the ball, carries him into his opponents' In-goal and he first there grounds the ball, even though it touched the ground in the field-of-play,

d) if a player first grounds the ball on his opponents' goal line or if the ball is in contact with the ground and a goal post.

(3) If a player grounds the ball in his opponents' In-goal and picks it up again, a try is scored where it was first grounded.

(4) A try may be scored by a player who is in touch or in touch-in-goal provided he is not carrying the ball.

B. Penalty Try.

A penalty try shall be awarded between the posts if but for obstruction, unfair play, foul play or misconduct by the defending team

- a try would probably have been scored, or
- it would probably have been scored in a more favorable position than that where the ball was grounded.

C.   Touch-Down.

(1) A touch-down occurs when a player first grounds the ball in his In-goal.

(2) After a touch-down, play shall be restarted either by a drop-out or a scrummage, as provided in Law 14.

D.   Scrummage after Grounding in Case of Doubt.

Where there is doubt as to which team first grounded the ball in In-goal, a scrummage shall be formed five meters from the goal line opposite the place where the ball was grounded. The attacking team shall put in the ball.

Law 13. Kick at Goal After a Try.

(1) After a try has been scored, the scoring team has the right to take a place kick or drop kick at goal, on a line through the place where the try was scored.
If the scoring team does not take the kick, play shall be restarted by a drop kick from the center, unless time has expired.

(2) If a kick is taken:—

a)   it must be taken without undue delay;

b)   any player including the kicker may place the ball;

c)   the **kicker's team**, except the placer, must be behind the ball when kicked;

d)   if the kicker kicks the ball from a placer's hands without the ball being on the ground, the kick is void;

e)   the **opposing team** must be behind the goal line until the kicker begins his run or offers to kick when they may charge or jump with a view to preventing a goal.

Penalty;

- For an infringement by the **kicker's team**—the kick shall be disallowed.

- For an infringement by the **opposing team**—the charge shall be disallowed. If, however, the kick has been taken successfully, the goal shall stand. If it was unsuccessful, the kicker may take another kick under the original conditions without the charge and may change the type of kick.

Neither the kicker nor a placer shall willfully do anything which may lead the opposing team to charge prematurely. If either does so, the charge shall not be disallowed.

NOTES

i   In addition to the general provision regarding waste of time, the kicker is bound to kick without delay, under penalty.

A player should not be permitted to be unreasonably slow in taking any kick at goal. A period of one minute between the indication of intention to kick at goal and the actual kick is well inside the zone of "undue delay." A player who is unreasonably slow should be warned that if he persists in delay, penalties will be applied.

Even without a caution, if the delay is clearly a breach of law, the kick should be disallowed and a kick-off ordered.

ii   The referee must always make up time lost by any delay in taking the kick, as is provided for in note (ii) under Law 5.

iii   The referee should see that the opposing players do not gradually creep up and that they have both feet behind the goal line, otherwise he should disallow the charge.

iv   Shouting by the defending team during a kick at goal should be treated as misconduct and, if no goal is scored, another kick should be allowed without the charge.

v   When another kick is allowed for any reason, all the original preliminaries may be retaken.

vi   If the ball rolls over and away from the line through the place where the try was scored and the ball is kicked over the crossbar, a goal should be awarded.

vii   If, after the kicker has commenced his run, the ball rolls over into touch, another kick under the original conditions should **not** be allowed.

viii   The kick must be taken with the ball which was in play unless the referee decides that the ball is defective.

ix   The law does not allow the use of sand or sawdust for placing the ball on hard playing fields when taking a place kick at goal, but in exceptional local conditions such a variation from normal practice might be permitted.

Law 14. In-Goal.

In-goal is the area bounded by a goal line, touch-in-goal lines and dead-ball line. It includes the goal line and goal posts but excludes touch-in-goal lines and dead-ball line.

Touch-in-goal occurs when the ball touches or crosses a touch-in-goal line or when the ball, or a player carrying it, touches a corner post, a touch-in-goal line or the ground beyond it. The flag is not part of the corner post.

Five Meters Scrummage

(1) If a player carrying the ball in In-goal is so held that he cannot ground the ball, a scrummage shall be formed five meters from the goal line opposite the place where he was held.
The attacking team shall put in thc ball.

(2) a) If a defending player heels, kicks, carries, passes or knocks the ball over his goal line and it there becomes dead except where

- a try is scored, or

- he willfully knocks or throws the ball from the field-of-play into touch-in-goal or over his dead-ball line, or

b) if a defending player in In-goal has his kick charged down by an attacking player after

- he carried the ball back from the field-of-play, or

- a defending player put it into In-goal and the ball is then touched down or goes into touch-in-goal or over the dead-ball line, or

c) if a defending player carrying the ball in the field-of-play is forced into his In-goal and he then touches down, or

d) if, at a scrummage or ruck, a defending team with the ball in its possession is pushed over its goal line and before the ball has emerged first grounds it in In-goal,

a scrummage shall be formed five meters from the goal line opposite the place where the ball or a player carrying it crossed the goal line. The attacking team shall put in the ball.

NOTES

i   If a defending player willfully puts the ball back into his own In-goal, he accepts **all** the consequences of taking that action. Many things may happen in In-goal after the ball has been carried, passed, knocked, heeled or kicked back by a defending player and it may be quite an appreciable time before the ball becomes dead and Law 14 applies.

ii   Paragraph 2 (b) of Law 14 applies whether the attacking player charges down the kick in the field-of-play or in In-goal.

iii   If play similar to a maul takes place in In-goal, Law 14 (1) applies.

Drop-Out.

(3) Except where a try or goal is scored, if an attacking player kicks, carries, passes or knocks the ball and it travels into his opponents' In-goal either directly or after having touched a defender who does not willfully attempt to stop, catch or kick it, and it is there

- grounded by a player of **either** team, or

- goes into touch-in-goal or over the dead-ball line

a drop-out shall be awarded.

Penalties

a)   A penalty try shall be awarded when by obstruction, unfair play, foul play or misconduct in In-goal the defending team has pre-vented a try which otherwise would *probably have been scored.*

b)   A try shall be disallowed and a drop-out awarded, if a try would *probably not* have been gained but for obstruction, unfair play, foul play or misconduct by the attacking team.

c)   For obstruction, unfair play, foul play or misconduct in In-goal while the ball is out of play the penalty kick shall be awarded at the place where play would otherwise have restarted and, in ad-dition, the player shall either be ordered off or cautioned that he will be sent off if he repeats the offense.

d)   For willfully charging or obstructing in In-goal a player who has just kicked the ball the penalty shall be

- a drop-out, or, at the option of the non-offending team,

- a penalty kick where the ball alights as provided for an infringement of Law 26 (3) (d).

e)   for other infringements in In-goal, the penalty shall be:—

- for an offense by the **attacking team**—a drop-out,

- for an offense by the **defending team**— scrummage five meters from the goal line opposite the place of infringement.

NOTES

iv   The decisions open to the referee for infringements in In-goal are:—

a) For an offense by the attacking team—
 * a drop-out, or
 * warning and/or sending off the player for foul play or misconduct, or
 * a penalty kick for obstruction, unfair play, foul play or misconduct in In-goal while the ball is out of play.

b) For an offense by the defending team—
 * a five meters scrummage, or
 * a penalty try, or
 * warning and/or sending off the player for foul play or misconduct, or
 * a penalty kick for obstruction, unfair play, foul play or misconduct in In-goal while the ball is out of play.

v   A penalty kick must **not** be awarded for an offense in In-goal except **only** when either Law 14 Penalty (d) or Law 26 (3) (h) applies. In the latter case the penalty kick is to be taken either at the twenty-two meters line [twenty-five yards line] (at any point the non-offending team may select) or at the center of the half-way line, whichever is the place where play would restart.

Law 15. Drop-Out.

A drop-out is a drop kick awarded to the defending team.

(1) The drop kick must be taken from anywhere on or behind the twenty-two meters line [twenty-five yards line]; otherwise the ball shall be dropped out again.

(2) The ball must reach the twenty-two meters line; otherwise the opposing team may have it dropped out again, or have a scrummage formed at the center of the twenty-two meters line. If it reaches the twenty-two meters line and is then blown back, play shall continue.

NOTE

i   If the ball does not reach the twenty-two meters line and an opponent picks up the ball and grounds it over the kicker's goal line, a try should be awarded.

(3) If the ball pitches directly into touch, the opposing team may accept the kick, have the ball dropped out again, or have a scrummage formed at the center of the twenty-two meters line.

(4) The **kicker's team** must be behind the ball when kicked; otherwise a scrummage shall be formed at the center of the twenty-two meters line.

(5) The **opposing team** must not charge over the twenty-two meters line; otherwise the ball shall be dropped out again.

NOTES

ii   If a player of the opposing team remains beyond or crosses the twenty-two meters line for the purpose of delaying or interfering with the player who is about to drop-out, a penalty under Law 26 (3) (h) should be awarded.

iii   The advantage law applies where the drop-kick does not reach the twenty-two meters line and goes into touch.

Law 16. Fair Catch (Mark).

a)   *A player makes a fair-catch when being stationary with both feet on the ground on his side of the halfway line he cleanly catches the ball direct from a kick, knock-on or throw-forward by one of his opponents and, at the same time, he exclaims "Mark!"*
A fair-catch may be obtained even though the ball on its way touches a goal post or crossbar and can be made in In-goal.

b)   *A free kick is awarded for a fair-catch.*

(1)   The kick must be taken by the player making the fair catch, unless he is injured in so doing. If he is unable to take the kick within two minutes a scrummage shall be formed at the mark. His team shall put in the ball.

(2)   If the mark is in In-goal, it shall be deemed to be on the goal line and the ball must cross that line unless first played by an opponent. Any resultant scrummage shall be five meters from the goal line on a line through the mark.

NOTE

i   'His side of the half-way line' means that no part of either foot is on or beyond the halfway line.

ii   If an opponent unfairly charges the catcher in the field-of-play after the referee has blown his whistle for a fair-catch, a penalty shall be awarded. If the charge occurs in In-goal, a drop out shall be awarded.

Law 17. Knock-On or Throw-Forward.

A knock-on occurs when a player propels the ball with his hand or arm in the direction of his opponents' dead-ball line or when the ball after striking the hand or arm of a player travels in that direction.

A throw-forward occurs when a player carrying the ball throws or passes it in the direction of his opponents' dead-ball line. A thrown-in from touch is not a throw-forward. If the ball is not thrown or passed forward but it bounces forward after hitting a player or the ground, it is not a throw-forward.

NOTES

i A pass, throw or knock-on should not be adjudged an infringement unless it is clearly so under the Law. If the ball in a player's possession is dislodged when he is tackled or falls to the ground, this is not propelling the ball forward. If there is any doubt, play should be allowed to proceed.

ii A fair-catch can be made from a knock-on.

(1) The knock-on or throw-forward must not be **intentional.**

Penalty: Penalty kick at the place of infringement.

(2) If the knock-on or throw-forward is **unintentional**, a scrummage shall be formed either at the place of infringement or, if it occurs at a lineout, fifteen meters from the touch line along the line-of-touch unless:—

• a fair catch has been allowed, or

• the ball is knocked on by a player who is in the act of charging down the kick of an opponent but is not attempting to catch the ball, or

• the ball is knocked on one or more times by a player who is in the act of catching or picking it up and is recovered by that player before it has touched the ground or another player.

NOTES

iii If an attacking player knocks-on in the field-of-play and the ball travels into In-goal, either directly or after having touched a defender who does not willfully attempt to stop, catch or kick it, and it is there

a) grounded by a player of either team, or
b) goes into touch-in-goal or over the dead-ball line,

a drop-out should be awarded.

Law 18. Tackle.

A tackle occurs when a player carrying the ball in the field-of-play is held by one or more opponents so that while he is so held the ball touches the ground.

(1) A tackled player, if lying on the ground, must release the ball immediately **without playing it in any other way** and get up or move away from it. He must not play or interfere with the ball in any way until he has got up on his feet.

NOTE

i   If a tackled player does not release the ball immediately and the referee is in doubt as to responsibility for failure to release it, he should **at once** order a scrummage.

(2) It is illegal for any player:—

- to prevent a tackled player from releasing the ball, or getting up after he has released it, or

- to attempt to pick up the ball before a tackled player lying on the ground has released it or to pull the ball from that player's possession,

- while lying on the ground after a tackle to play or interfere with the ball in any way. Nevertheless while still lying on the ground *any* player may tackle or attempt to tackle an opponent carrying the ball.

Penalty:—Penalty kick at the place of infringement.

(3) If a player carrying the ball is thrown or knocked over but not tackled, he may pass the ball or get up and continue his run even though the ball has touched the ground.

(4) A try may be scored if the momentum of a player carries him into his opponents' In-goal even though he is held.

NOTES

ii   A ruck has been formed if players of both teams are in physical contact in close proximity around the ball on the ground after a tackle. If the ball is played with the hands or picked up before it emerges from the ruck, a penalty kick should be awarded.

iii Danger may arise if a tackled player on the ground fail to release or roll away from the ball at once or is prevented from doing so. In such cases **the referee should not delay awarding a penalty kick**.

Law 19. Lying On or Near the Ball.

A player who is lying on the ground and

a)   is holding the ball, or

b)   is preventing an opponent from gaining possession of it, or

c)   has fallen on or over the ball emerging from a scrummage or ruck,

must **immediately** play the ball or get up or roll away from it.

Penalty:—Penalty kick at the place of infringement.

Law 20. Scrummage.

A scrummage, which can take place only in the field-of-play, is formed by players from each team closing up in readiness to allow the ball to be put on the ground between them.

The middle player in each front row is the hooker, and the players on either side of him are the props.

The middle line means an imaginary line of the ground directly beneath the line formed by the junction of the shoulders of the two front rows.

NOTE

If the ball in a scrummage is on or over the goal line the scrummage is ended.

Forming a Scrummage

(1) A team must not willfully delay the forming of a scrummage.

(2) Every scrummage shall be formed at the place of infringement or as near thereto as is practicable within the field-of-play. It must be stationary with the middle line parallel to the goal lines until the ball has been put in.

NOTE

i　To the extent that is necessary, the scrummage is to be moved from the place of infringement so that

a) when it is near a goal line, the line of the front row of the defending team, or

b) when near a touch line, the whole of the scrummage is the field-of-play before the ball is put in.

The scrummage is ended if the ball in the scrummage touches or crosses a goal line.

(3) It is dangerous play for a front row to form down some distance from its opponents and rush against them.

(4) Each front row of a scrummage shall have three players in it **at all times.** Subject to this, any number of players may form a scrummage. The head of a player in a font row shall not be next to the head of a player of the same team.

(5) While a scrummage is forming and is taking place, all players in each front row must adopt a normal stance. Both feet must be on the ground, must not be crossed and must be in the position for an effective forward shove.

NOTES

ii   The restriction on the crossing of the feet of the players in the front rows refers only to the feet of individual players; but the feet of all players in the front rows "must be in the position for an effective forward shove."

iii   A flank forward in the second or third row of a scrummage may pack at an angle provided he is properly bound. If the ball is emerging from the back of the scrummage and he moves outwards, thereby preventing an an opponent from advancing around the scrummage, a penalty kick should be awarded.

Binding of Players

(6) a)   The players of each front row shall bind firmly and continuously while the ball is being put in and while it is in the scrummage.

b)   The hooker may bind either over or under the arms of his props but, in either case, he must bind firmly around their bodies at or below the level of the armpits. The props must bind the hooker similarly. The hooker must not be supported so that he is not carrying any weight on either foot.

c)   The near prop of the team putting in the ball must bind with his outside arm inside the arm of the near prop of the opposing team. The far prop of the team not putting in the ball must bind similarly with the far prop of the opposing team.

d)   All players in a scrummage, other than those in a front row, must bind with at least one arm and hand around the body of another player of the same team.

e)   Any outside player other than a prop may hold an opponent with his outer arm but only to keep himself and the scrummage steady. He must not push or pull an opponent or his dress.

Putting the Ball into the Scrummage

(7)   The team not responsible for the stoppage of play shall put in the ball. In the event of doubt as to responsibility the ball shall be put in by the team which was moving forward prior to the stoppage or, if neither team was moving forward, by the defending team.

NOTE

iv   A stoppage may be caused without any infringement by either team.
The words "responsible for the stoppage of play" include legitimate actions by a team, such as falling on the ball, tackling, etc., which prevent the opposing team from continuing play.

(8) The ball shall be put in without delay as soon as the two front rows have closed together. A team must put in the ball when ordered to do so and on the side first chosen.

NOTE

    v   The referee has no authority to permit delay in putting in the ball because a player has not succeeded in getting his head down in the scrummage.

        A penalty kick should be awarded if the referee is satisfied that the delay by the team in putting the ball in is deliberate and prejudices the other team.

(9) The player putting in the ball shall

    a)   stand **one** meter from the scrummage and midway between the two front rows;

    b)   hold the ball with both hands midway between the two front rows at a level midway between his knee and ankle;

    c)   from that position put in the ball

        • without any delay or without feint or backward movement, i.e. with a single forward movement, and

        • at a quick speed straight along the middle line so that it first touches the ground immediately beyond the width of the nearer prop's shoulders.

(10) If the ball is put in and it comes out at either end of the tunnel, it shall be put in again, unless a free kick or penalty kick has been awarded.

If the ball comes out otherwise than at either end of the tunnel and if a penalty kick has not been awarded play shall proceed.

NOTE

    vi The advantage law applies as soon as the ball has left the hands of the player putting it into the scrummage.

Restrictions on Front Row Players

(11) All front row players must place their feet so as to allow a clear tunnel. A player must not prevent the ball from being put into the scrummage, or from touching the ground at the required place.

(12) No front row player may raise or advance a foot until the ball has touched the ground.

NOTE

    vii Until any foot is permitted to be raised or advanced, that foot must be kept in the normal position.

(13) When the ball has touched the ground, any foot of any player in either front row may be used in an attempt to gain possession of the ball subject to the following:—

players in the front rows must not **at any time** during the scrummage:—

a) raise both feet off the ground at the same time, or

b) willfully adopt any position or willfully take any action, by twisting or lowering the body or otherwise, which is likely to cause the scrummage to collapse, or

c) willfully kick the ball out of the tunnel in the direction from which it is put in.

NOTES

viii The prohibition against a player in the front row raising both feet off the ground at the same time or striking at the ball with both feet applies during the whole scrummage and not merely to the period while the ball is being put in.

ix Referees must be strict in applying penalties for willfully kicking out. Repeated kicking out **must** be treated as willful.

x When the referee orders the ball to be put in again it must be put in by a player of the same team that was first entitled to do so.

xi If the ball is about to pass straight through the tunnel and a far prop advances a foot so that the ball passes behind that foot, the ball must be put in again unless it has been lawfully played, (i.e. touched) by a player in the front row.

Restrictions on Players

(14) Any player who is not in either front row must not play the ball while it is in the tunnel.

(15) A player must not:—

a) return the ball into the scrummage, or

b) handle the ball in the scrummage except in the act of obtaining a "push over" try or touch-down, or

c) pick up the ball in the scrummage by hand or legs, or

d) willfully collapse the scrummage, or

e) willfully fall or kneel in the scrummage.

NOTE

xii Referees must be strict in penalizing for the willful collapsing of scrummage as stated under Law 20 (15) (d) and Law 26 (3) (g).

(16) The player putting in the ball and his immediate opponent must not kick the ball while it is in the scrummage.

NOTE

xiii If a player repeatedly infringes, he must be dealt with under Law 26 (3).

Penalty:—

a) For an infringement of paragraphs (2), (5), (8), (9), (11), (12) and (14), a free kick at the place of infringement.

b) For an infringement of paragraphs (1), (3), (4), (6), (13), (15) and (16), a penalty kick at the place of infringement.

For Off-side at Scrummage see Law 24B.

Law 21. Ruck.

A ruck, which can take place only in the field-of-play, is formed when the ball is on the ground and one or more players from each team are on their feet and in physical contact, closing around the ball between them.

NOTE

If the ball in a ruck is on or over the goal line the ruck is ended.

(1) A player joining a ruck must bind with at least one arm around the body of a player of his team in the ruck.

NOTE

i The placing of a hand on another player is not binding. Binding involves the whole arm, from hand to shoulder.

(2) A player must not:—

a) return the ball into the ruck, or

b) handle the ball in the ruck except in the act of securing a try or touch-down, or

c) pick up the ball in the ruck by hand or legs, or

d) willfully collapse the ruck, or

e) jump on top of other players in the ruck, or

f) willfully fall or kneel in the ruck, or

g) while lying on the ground interfere in any way with the ball in or emerging from the ruck. He must do his best to roll away from it.

Penalty:—Penalty kick at the place of infringement.

For Off-side at Ruck see Law 24C.

Law 22. Maul.

A maul, which can take place only in the field-of-play, is formed by one or more players from each team on their feet and in physical contact closing around a player who is carrying the ball.

A maul ends when the ball is on the ground or the ball or a player carrying it emerges from the maul or when a scrummage is ordered.

NOTE

If the ball on a maul is on or over the goal line the maul is ended.

(1) A player is not in physical contact unless he is caught in or bound to the maul and not merely alongside it.

(2) A player must not jump on top of other players in the maul.

(3) When the ball in a maul becomes unplayable a scrummage shall be ordered and the team which was moving forward immediately prior to the stoppage shall put in the ball, or if neither team was moving forward, the defending team shall put it in.

NOTE

i   Before whistling for a scrummage, the referee should allow a reasonable time for the ball to emerge from the maul, particularly if either team is moving forward. If in his opinion the ball will probably not emerge from the maul without delay, he should not allow prolonged wrestling for the ball but should order a scrummage.

Penalty:—Penalty kick at the place of infringement.

For Off-side at Maul see Law 24D.

Law 23. Touch and Line-Out.

A. Touch.

(1) The ball is in touch

- when it is not being carried by a player and it touches or crosses a touch line, or

- when it is being carried by a player and it or the player carrying it touches a touch line or the ground beyond it.

Exception:—

If a player in the field-of-play catches the ball immediately after it has crossed the touch line it is not in touch provided the player does not go into touch.

(2) If the ball crosses a touch line and then comes back, it is in touch at the place where it first crossed the line.

(3) If the ball is not in touch a player who is in touch may kick the ball or propel it with his hand but not hold it.

NOTES

i   a) If the ball pitches directly into touch from a kickoff and the opposing side elects to accept the kick, the line-out shall be formed

   • at the half-way line, or

   • where the ball crosses the touch line if that place be nearer to the kicker's goal-line.

   b) If the ball pitches directly into touch from a dropout and the opposing team elects to accept the kick, the line-out shall be formed where the ball went into touch.

   c) "pitching directly into touch" means that the ball, having been kicked, first touches the ground on or beyond a touch line **and** has not touched or been touched in flight by an opponent or the referee.

   d) If the ball, having been kicked, crosses a touch line and then comes back into the field-of-play, it is deemed to have pitched in touch at the place where it first crossed the touch line.

ii   It is **not** touch when a player with both feet in the field-of-play catches the ball, even though the ball before being caught has crossed the touch line. This does not apply if before being caught the ball has touched the touch line or the ground beyond, or has previously crossed the touch line and come back, or has been in touch for some distance before being caught. The ball first crossing the touch line and the player catching it must occur in quick sequence.

B. Line-Out.

The line-of-touch is an imaginary line in the field of play at right angles to the touch line through the place where the ball is to be thrown in.

Formation of Line-Out

(1) A line-out is formed by at least two players from each team lining up in single lines parallel to the line-of-touch in readiness for the ball to

be thrown in between them. Players who so line up are those "in the line-out," unless excluded below.

NOTE

iii Prior to the beginning of the line-out, any offense, including willfully failing to form a line-out, or to line up at least two players, should be dealt with as misconduct under Law 26 (3) (h).

(2) Each player in the line-out must stand at least one meter from the next player of his team in the line-out.

NOTE

iv The distance of "at least one meter" means between players who are deemed to be facing the touch line and standing upright with their feet together. Players may adopt any stance and face in any direction.

(3) The line-out stretches from five meters from the touch line from which the ball is being thrown to the position at the time the line-out begins of the farthest player in the line-out of the team throwing in the ball, but the furthest player must not be more than fifteen meters from that touch line.

(4) Any player of either team who is farther from the touch line than the position of the farthest player when the line-out begins is NOT in the line-out.

(5) A clear space of 500 millimeters must be left between the two lines of players.

NOTES

v The distance of 500 millimeters for the clear space is between the shoulders of the players when standing upright.

vi If, at a formed line-out, the team throwing in the ball line up less than the normal number, their opponents must be given a reasonable opportunity to conform to the established length of the line-out. Opposing players who are retiring for that purpose must do so directly and without delay to a line ten meters behind the line-of-touch. Loiterers must be penalized. Subject to this, when the line-out is ended players so retiring may rejoin play, even if they have not reached the ten meters line.

Throwing in the Ball

(6) When the ball is in touch the place at which it must be thrown in is as follows:—

• when the ball goes into touch from a penalty kick, free kick, or from a kick within twenty-two meters of the kicker's goal line, at the place where the ball went into touch, or

- when the ball pitches directly into touch after having been kicked otherwise than as stated above, opposite the place from which the ball was kicked or at the place where it went into touch if that place be nearer to the kicker's goal line, or

- on all other occasions when the ball is in touch, at the place where the ball went into touch.

(7) The ball must be thrown at the line-out by an opponent of the player whom it last touched, or by whom it was carried, before being in touch. In the event of doubt as to which team should throw in the ball, the defending team shall do so.

(8) The player must throw in the ball

- at the place indicated, and

- so that it touches the ground or touches or is touched by a player at least five meters from the touch line along the line-of-touch, and

- while throwing in the ball, he must not put any part of either foot in the field-of-play.

If any of the foregoing is infringed, the opposing team shall have the right, at its option, to throw in the ball or to take a scrummage.

If on the second occasion the ball is not thrown in correctly a scrummage shall be formed and the ball shall be put it in by the team which threw it in on the first occasion.

NOTES

vii If a player willfully prevents the ball from being thrown in five meters, a penalty kick should be awarded.

viii If a player willfully throws the ball in not straight a penalty kick should be awarded.

(9) **A quick throw-in** from touch without waiting for the players to form a line-out is permissible provided the ball that went into touch is used, it has been handled only by the players and it is thrown in correctly.

NOTE

ix At a quick throw-in the farthest player and fifteen meters from touch requirements do not apply.

Beginning and End of Line-out

(10) The line-out begins when the ball leaves the hands of the player throwing it in.

(11) The line-out ends when

- a ruck or maul is taking place and all feet of players in the ruck or maul have moved beyond the line-of-touch, or

- a player carrying the ball leaves the line-out, or

- the ball has been passed, knocked back or kicked from the line-out, or

- the ball is thrown beyond the farthest player, or

- the ball becomes unplayable.

NOTES (I.R.F.B. NOTES 12 & 14)

x   If a player participating in a line-out hands the ball to another player who is peeling-off from the line-out, the line-out ends when the second player takes the ball.

xi   A ruck or maul has not moved from the line-of-touch unless all the feet of the players in the ruck or maul have moved beyond that line.

Peeling Off

"Peeling off" occurs when a player (or players) moves from his position in the line-out for the purpose of catching the ball when it has been passed or knocked back by another of his team in the line-out.

(12) When the ball is in touch players who approach the line-of-touch must **always** be presumed to do so for the purpose of forming a line-out. Except in a peeling off movement such players must not leave the line-of-touch, or the line-out when formed, until the line-out has ended.

Exceptions:—

i)   At a quick throw-in, when a player may come to the line-of-touch and retire from that position without penalty.

ii) When the team throwing in the ball line up less than the normal number of players, opposing players in excess of the reduced number may retire without penalty, provided they do so without delay and to their off-side line as defined at the head of Law 24E.

(13) A player must not begin to peel off until the ball has left the hands of the player throwing it in. He must move parallel and close to the line-out. If the line-out does not end he must rejoin it.

Restrictions on Players in Line-out

(14) **Before** the ball has been thrown in and has touched the ground or has touched or been touched by a player, any player in the line-out must not

a)   be off-side, or

b   push, charge, shoulder or bind with or in any way hold another player of either team, or

c)   use any other player as a support to enable him to jump for the ball, or

d)   stand within five meters of the touch line or prevent the ball from being thrown five meters.

NOTES (I.R.F.B. NOTES 10, 11, 13)

xii Any movement of a player beyond the length of the line-out as established by the furthest player must be solely for the purpose of catching or jumping to catch the ball. The player may move in-field in an attempt to catch the ball only after it leaves the hand of the player throwing it in and it is thrown beyond the position of the farthest player.

xiii A player acting as scrum-half may not stand or move beyond the farthest player before the ball has passed that player unless he moves to anticipate a long throw-in but he may so move only in accordance with the conditions in the preceding note xii

xiv When the ball has been passed or knocked back from a line-out, the line-out is ended. Players in front of a player of their own team who receives the ball from the line-out may be off-side but they should only be penalized under Law 24A if they play the ball or obstruct an opponent in any way.

(15) **After** the ball has touched the ground or touched or been touched by a player, any player in the line-out must not

a)   be off-side, or

b)   hold, push, shoulder or obstrust an opponent not holding the ball, or

c)   charge an opponent except in an attempt to tackle him or play the ball.

(16) Except when jumping for the ball or peeling off, each player in the line-out must remain at least one meter from the next player of his team until the ball has touched or has been touched by a player or has touched the ground.

(17) Except when jumping for the ball or peeling off, a clear space of 500 millimeters [two feet] must be left between the two lines of players until the ball has touched or has been touched by a player or has touched the ground.

NOTE

xv The act of jumping for the ball can include a step if it is a simple movement in endeavouring to catch the ball.

(18) A player in the line-out may move into the space between the touch line and the five meters mark only when the ball has been thrown beyond him and, if he does so, he must not move towards his goal line before the line-out ends, except in a peeling off movement.

(19) Until the line-out ends, no player may be or move beyond the position of the farthest player when the line out begins except as allowed when the ball is thrown beyond that position, in accordance with the Exception following law 24E (1) (d). If the farthest player moves toward the touch line after the ball has been thrown in, other players in the line-out are not required to follow him in order to remain on-side.

NOTE

xvi If the ball in a line-out becomes unplayable, otherwise than as a result of an infringement for which a penalty is prescribed, a scrummage should be ordered.

Penalty:— A penalty kick fifteen meters from the touch line along the line-of-touch.

Restrictions on Players not in Line-Out

(20) Players of either team who are not in line-out may not advance from behind the line-out and take the ball from the throw-in except only

- a player at a quick throw-in, or

- a player advancing at a long throw-in, or

- a player "participating in the line-out" (as defined in Section E of Law 24) who may run into a gap in the line-out and take the ball provided he does not charge or obstruct any player in the line-out.

Penalty:—

a) For an infringement of paragraphs (1), (2), (3), (4), (5), (12), (16), (17), or (187) a free kick fifteen meters from the touch line along the line-of-touch.

b) For an infringement of paragraphs (13), (14), (15), or (19), a penalty kick fifteen meters from the touch line along the line-of-touch.

c) For an infringement of paragraph (20), a penalty kick on the offending team's off-side line (as defined in Law 24E opposite the place of infringement, but not less than fifteen meters from the touch line.

Place on scrummage: Any scrummage taken or ordered under this Law or as the result of any infringement in a line-out shall be formed fifteen meters from the touch line along the line-of-touch.

For Off-side at Line-Out see Law 24E.

NOTE

xvii If a player repeatedly infringes, he **must** be dealt with under Law 26 (3).

Law 24. Off-Side.

Off-side means that a player is in a position in which he is out of the game and is liable to penalty.

In general play the player is in an off-side position because he is in front of the ball when it has been last played by another player of his team.

In play at scrummage, ruck, maul or line-out the player is off-side because he remains or advances in front of the line or line or place stated in, or otherwise infringes, the relevant sections of this Law.

A. Off-side in General Play.

(1) A player is an off-side position if the ball has been
- kicked, or

- touched, or

- is being carried

by one of his team behind him.

(2) there is no penalty for being in an off-side position unless:—

a) the player plays the ball or obstructs an opponent, or

b) he approaches or remains within ten meters of an opponent waiting to play the ball.

Where no opponent is waiting to play the ball but one arrives as the ball pitches, a player in an off-side position must not obstruct or interfere with him.

Exceptions:—

1) When an off-side player cannot avoid being touched by the ball or by a player carrying it, he is "accidentally off-side." Play should be allowed to continue unless the infringing team obtains an advantage, in which case a scrummage should be formed at that place.

ii A player who receives an unintentional throw-forward is not off-side.

iii If, because of the speed of the game, an off-side player finds himself unavoidably within ten meters of an opponent waiting to play the ball, he shall not be penalized provided he retires without delay and without interfering with the opponent.

Penalty:—Penalty kick at the place of infringement, or at the option of the nonoffending team, a scrummage at the place where the ball was last played by the offending team. If the latter place is In-goal, the scrummage shall be formed five meters from the goal line on a line through the place.

NOTES

i   A penalty for off-side should not be given at once if the non-offending team gains an advantage or if it appears likely to gain an advantage: but if the expected advantage is not gained, the penalty should in all cases be awarded even if it is necessary to bring play back for that purpose to the place of infringement.

ii   When a player knocks on and an off-side player of the same team next plays the ball, a penalty for off-side should not be awarded unless the off-side deprives the nonoffending team of an advantage.

iii A player can be off-side in his In-goal.

iv   If a player hands the ball to another player of his team in front of him, the second player is off-side. A scrummage for "accidental off-side" should be awarded unless it is considered the player was willfully off-side in which case a penalty kick should be awarded.

v   The referee should whistle at once if an off-side player who cannot be placed on-side charges within ten meters of an opponent waiting to receive the ball. Delay may prove dangerous to the latter player.

     Where there is no opponent **waiting** to play the ball but one arrives as the ball pitches, an off-side player who is near such opponent must not obstruct or interfere with him in any way whatsoever before he is put on-side.

vi   If an attacking player kicks the ball which is misfielded by an opponent and the ball is then played by another attacking player in an off-side position within ten meters of the opponent, a penalty kick should be awarded.

vii If an atacking player kicks the ball which is charged down by an opponent and another attacking player within ten meters of the opponent then plays the ball, play should be allowed to continue. The opponent was not "waiting to play the ball" and the second attacking player is therefore on-side under Law 25 (2).

viii If a defending player is waiting to play the ball after it has rebounded from a goal post or crossbar, Law 24 A (2) (b) applies to off-side players of the attacking team who are within ten meters of that defending player.

B. Off-side at Scrummage.

The term "off-side line" means a line parallel to the goal lines through the hindmost foot of the player's team in the scrummage.

While a scrummage is forming or is taking place:—

(1) a player is off-side if

   a)   he joins it from his opponents' side, or

   b)   he, not being in the scrummage nor the player of either team who puts the ball in the scrummage,

      • fails to retire behind the off-side line or to his goal line whichever is the nearer, or

      • places either foot in front of the off-side line while the ball is in the scrummage.

   A player behind the ball may leave a scrummage provided he retires immediately behind the off-side line.

   If he wishes to rejoin the scrumage, he must do so behind the ball.

   He may not play the ball as it emerges between the feet of his front row if he is in front of the off-side line.

Exception:—the restrictions on leaving the scrummage in front of the off-side line do not apply to a player taking part in "wheeling" a scrummage.

(2) A player is off-side if he, being a player of either team who puts the ball in the scrummage, remains, or places either foot, in front of the ball while it is in the scrummage, or if he is the immediate opponent of the player putting in the ball, takes up position on the opposite side of the scrummage in front of the off-side line.

Penalty:— Penalty kick at the place of infringement.

NOTES

  ix   Players must retire without delay to the scrummage off-side line when a scrummage is forming. Loiterers must be penalized.

  x   Any player of either team may at a particular scrummage be the player who puts in the ball or who takes up position as scrum half when his opponent is putting in the ball: but such player is at that scrummage the only player of his team who has the benefit of Law 24 B (2).

C. Off-side at Ruck.

The term "off-side line" means a line parallel to the goal lines through the hindmost foot of the player's team in the ruck.

(1) Ruck otherwise than at line-out

While a ruck is taking place, a player is off-side if he:—

   a) joins it from his opponents' side, or

   b) joins it in front of the ball, or

   c) does not join the ruck but fails to retire behind the off-side line **without delay,** or

   d) advances beyond the off-side line with either foot and does not join the ruck, or

   e) unbinds from the ruck and does not **immediately** either rejoin it behind the ball or retire behind the off-side line.

   Penalty:—Penalty kick at the place of infringement.

(2) Ruck at line-out

The term "participating in the line-out" has the same meaning as in Section E of this Law. A player participating in the line-out is not obliged to join or remain in the ruck and if he is not in the ruck he continues to participate in the line-out until it has ended.

While a line-out is in progress and ruck takes place, a player is off-side if he:—

   a) joins the ruck from his opponents' side, or

   b) joins it in front of the ball, or

   c) being a player who is participating in the line out and is not in the ruck does, not retire to and remain at the off-side line defined in this section, or

   Penalty:—Penalty kick fifteen meters from the touch line along the line-of-touch.

   d) being a player who is not participating in the line-out, remains or advances with either foot in front of the off-side line defined in Section E of this Law.

   Penalty:—Penalty kick on the offending team's off-side line (as defined in Section E of this Law) opposite the place of infringement, but not less than fifteen meters from the touch line.

   NOTE

   xi When the line-out is ended but the ruck is still taking place, a player is off-side if he infringes Section C (1) of this Law.

D. Off-Side at Maul.

The term "off-side line" means a line parallel to the goal lines through the hindmost foot of the player's team in the maul.

(1) **Maul otherwise than at line-out**

While a maul is taking place (including a maul which continues after a line-out has ended), a player is off-side if he:

a)   joins it from his opponents' side, or

b)   joins it in front of the ball, or

c)   does not join the maul but fails to retire behind the off-side line without delay, or

d)   advances beyond the off-side line with either foot and does not join the maul, or

e)   leaves the maul and does not immediately either rejoin it behind the ball or retire behind the off-side line.

Penalty:—Penalty kick at the place of infringement.

(2) **Maul at line-out**

The term "participating in the line-out" has the same meaning as in Section E of this Law. A player participating in the line-out is not obliged to join or remain in the maul and if he is not in the maul he continues to participate in the line-out until it has ended.

While a line-out is in progress and a maul takes place, a player is off-side if he:

a)   joins the maul from his opponents' side, or

b)   joins it in front of the ball, or

c)   being a player who is participating in the line-out and is not in the maul, does not retire to and remain at the off-side line defined in this Section, or

Penalty:—Penalty kick fifteen meters from the touch line along the line-of-touch.

d)   being a player who is not participating in the line-out, remains or advances with either foot in front of the off-side line defined in Section E of this Law.

Penalty:—Penalty kick on the offending team's off-side line (as defined in Section E of this law) opposite the place of infringement, but not less than fifteen meters from the touch line.

NOTE

xi   When the line-out has ended but the maul is still taking place, a player is off-side if he infringes Section D (1) of this Law.

E.   Off-side at Line-out.

The term "participating in the line-out" refers exclusively to the following players:—

- *those players who are in the line-out, and*

- *the player who throws in the ball, and*

- *his immediate opponent who may have the option of throwing in the ball, and*

- *one other player of either team who takes up position to receive the ball if it is passed or knocked back from the line-out.*

All other players are not *participating in the line-out.*

The term "off-side line" means a line ten meters behind the line-of-touch and parallel to the goal lines or, if the goal line be nearer than ten meters to the line-of-touch, the "off-side line" is the goal line.

Off-side while participating in line-out.

(1) A participating player is off-side if:—

a) **before** the ball has touched a player or the ground he willfully remains or advances with either foot in front of the line-of-touch, unless he advances solely in the act of jumping for the ball, or

b) **after** the ball has touched a player or the ground, if he is not carrying the ball, he advances with either foot in front of the ball, unless he is lawfully tackling or attempting to tackle an opponent who is participating in the line-out. Such tackle or attempt to tackle must, however, start from his side of the ball, or

c) in a peeling off movement he fails to keep close to the line-out and, if the line-out does not end, he fails to rejoin it, or

d) before the line-out ends he

- ceases to participate in the line-out, or

- moves beyond the position of the farthest player.

Exception:—Players of the team throwing in the ball may move beyond the position of the farthest player for a long throw-in to them. They may do so only when the ball leaves the hands of the player throwing it in and if they do so their opponents participating in the line-out may follow them. If players so move and the ball is not thrown to or beyond them they must be penalized for off-side.

Penalty:—Penalty kick fifteen meters from the touch line along the line-of-touch.

NOTES (I.R.F.B. Notes 14, 15, & 16)

xii Players who advance beyond the off-side line or who move beyond the back-marker in the expectation of a long throw-in must be penalized if, for any reason, the ball is not thrown beyond the back-marker.

xiii A player jumping unsuccessfully for the ball who crosses the line-of-touch should be given an opportunity to retire before being penalized.

xiv The referee should be strict in dealing with those players who, while not disputing possession of the ball in the line-out, advance to an off-side position whether intentionally or not.

(2) The player throwing in the ball and his immediate opponent must:—

a)   remain within five meters of the touch line, or

b)   retire to the off-side line, or

c)   join the line-out after the ball has been thrown in five meters, or

d)   move into position to receive the ball if it is passed or knocked back from the line-out provided no other player is occupying that position at that line-out.

NOTE (I.R.F.B. Note 13)

xv   If a player other than the wing-threequarter throws in the ball from touch, the wing-threequarter must retire to the off-side line, or join the line-out.

Off-side while not participating in the line-out.

(3) A player who is not participating is off-side if before the line-out has ended he advances or remains with either foot in front of the off-side line.

Exception:—Players of the same team throwing in the ball who are not participating in the line-out may advance for a long throw-in to them beyond the line-out. They may do so only when the ball leaves the hand of the player throwing in the ball and, if they do, their opponents may advance to meet them. If players so advance for a long throw-in to them and the ball is not thrown to them they must be penalized for off-side.

NOTE (I.R.F.B. Note 12)

xvi If a player not participating in the line-out is off-side, the referee should not whistle immediately if the opposing team is likely to gain an advantage. He should apply the advantage law in all such cases.

(Note xii also applies)

Players returning to "on-side" position.

(4) A player is not obliged, before throwing in the ball, to wait until players of his team have returned to or behind the line-out but such players are off-side unless they return to an on-side position **without delay**.

Penalty:—Penalty kick on the offending team's off-side line (as defined in Section E of this Law) opposite the place of infringement, but not less than fifteen meters from the touch line.

NOTE TO LAWS 24 B, C, D and E.
OFF-SIDE AT SCRUMMAGE, RUCK, MAUL and LINE-OUT.

xvii Where these Laws state a line which determines the off-side position such line stretches continuously from touch line to touch line.

Law 25. On-Side.

On-side means that a player is in the Game and not liable to penalty for off-side.

Player made on-side by action of his team.

(1) Any player who is off-side in general play including an off-side player who is within ten meters of an opponent waiting to play the ball and is retiring as required, becomes on-side as a result of any of the following actions of his team:

- when the off-side player has retired behind the player of his team who last kicked, touched or carried the ball, or

- when one of his team carrying the ball has run in front of him, or

- when one of his team has run in front of him after coming from the place or from behind the place where the ball was kicked.

    In order to put the off-side player on-side, this other player must be in the field-of-play or in In-goal, but he is not debarred from following up in touch or touch-in-goal.

NOTE

i   An off-side player who is within ten meters of an opponent waiting to play the ball must retire and continue to do so up to ten meters until he is put on-side. If he does not do so, he must be penalized.

Player made on-side by action of opposing team.

(2) Any player who is off-side in general play, **except** an off-side player within ten meters of an opponent waiting to play the ball, becomes on-side as a result of any of the following actions:—

- when an opponent carrying the ball has run five meters, or

- when an opponent kicks or passes the ball, or

- when an opponent **intentionally** touches the ball and does not catch or gather it.

An off-side player within ten meters of an opponent waiting to play the ball **cannot** be put on-side by **any** action of his opponents. Any **other** off-side player in general play is **always** put on-side when an opponent plays the ball.

Player retiring at scrummage, ruck, maul or line-out.

(3) A player who is in an off-side position when a scrummage, ruck, maul or line-out is forming or taking place and is retiring as required by Law 24 (Off-side) becomes on-side:—

- when an opponent carrying the ball has run five meters, or

- when an opponent has kicked the ball.

An off-side player in this situation is not put on-side when an opponent passes the ball.

NOTES

ii   The referee should be careful to ensure that no benefit under Law 25 (2) is gained by loiterers who willfully remain in an off-side position and thereby prevent opponents from running with, kicking, passing or otherwise playing the ball.

iii   When a team has gained quick possession from a scrummage, ruck, maul or line-out and starts a passing movement, opponents who are retiring must not be allowed to interfere with the movement unless the conditions of Law 25 (3) exist. Referees should be strict in applying this.

Law 26. Obstruction, Unfair Play, Foul Play, Misconduct, Repeated Infringements.

Obstruction

(1) It is illegal for any player:—

a)   who is running for the ball to charge or push an opponent also running for the ball, except shoulder to shoulder,

b)   who is in an off-side position willfully to run or stand in front of another player of his team who is carrying the ball, thereby preventing an opponent from reaching the latter player,

c)   who is carrying the ball after it has come out of a scrummage, ruck, maul or line-out to attempt to force his way through the players of his team in front of him.

d)   who is an outside player from a scrummage or ruck to prevent an opponent from advancing round the scrummage or ruck.

Penalty:—Penalty kick at the place of infringement. A penalty try may be awarded.

NOTES

i   There are no circumstances in which a player carrying the ball can be penalized for obstruction.

ii   The referee should note that:
a) The intention of this Law as regards the penalties to be imposed for serious forms of obstruction must be applied.

b) If a player is guilty of charging or obstructing or holding an opponent who is not carrying the ball or any other form of foul play, before any other action is taken the player **must** at once be cautioned or sent off. If he offends a second time, the referee has no alternative to sending him off. If the offense prevents a try which **probably** would otherwise have been scored, a penalty try must be awarded.

c) The intention of the International Board is that if the referee has any doubt as to the balance of probability, he should give the benefit of the doubt in favor of the nonoffending team and award the penalty try.

Unfair Play

(2)   It is illegal for any player:—

a)   deliberately to play unfairly or willfully infringe any Law of the Game,

b)   willfully to waste time,

c)   willfully to knock or throw the ball from the field-of-play into touch, touch-in-goal or over his dead-ball line.

Penalty:—Penalty kick at the place of infringement. A penalty try may be awarded.

NOTE

iii   Unfair play is action or conduct which is contrary to the Object of the Game.

Foul Play, Misconduct and Repeated Infringements

(3)   It is illegal for any player:—

a)   to strike an opponent,

b)   willfully to hack or kick an opponent or trip him with the foot,

c)   to tackle early, or late or dangerously, including the action known as "a stiff arm tackle,"

d)   who is not running for the ball willfully to charge or obstruct an opponent who has just kicked the ball,

e) to hold, push, charge, obstruct or grasp an opponent not holding the ball except in a scrummage, ruck or maul,

(Except in a scrummage or ruck the dragging away of a player lying close to the ball is permitted. Otherwise pulling any part of the clothing of an opponent is holding.)

f) in the front row of a scrummage to form down some distance from the opponents and rush against them,

g) willfully to cause a scrummage or ruck to collapse,

h) while the ball is out of play to molest, obstruct or in any way interfere with an opponent or be guilty of any form of misconduct,

i) to infringe repeatedly any Law of the Game,

j) to commit any misconduct on the field-of-play which is prejudicial to the spirit of good sportsmanship.

Penalty:—A player guilty of foul play or misconduct shall either be ordered off or else cautioned that he will be sent off if he repeats the offense. For a similar offense after caution, the player must be sent off.

In addition to a caution or ordering off a penalty try or a penalty kick shall be awarded as follows:—

i) If the offense prevents a try which would otherwise **probably** have been scored, a penalty try shall be awarded.

ii) The place for a penalty kick shall be:—

a) For offenses other than under paragraphs (d) and (h), at the place of infringement.

b) For an infringement of (d) the nonoffending team shall have the option of taking the kick at the place of infringement or where the ball alights, and if the ball alights

- **in touch,** the mark is fifteen meters from the touch line on a line parallel to the goal lines through the place where it crossed the touch line, or

- **within fifteen meters from the touch line,** it is fifteen meters from the touch line on a line parallel to the goal lines through the place where it alighted, or

- **in In-goal, touch-in-goal, or over or on the dead-ball line,** it is five meters from the goal line on a line parallel to the touch line through the place where it crossed the goal line or fifteen meters from the touch line whichever is the greater.

c) For an offense under (h), at any place where the ball would next have been brought into play if the offense had not occurred, or, if that place is on the touch line, fifteen meters from that place, on a line parallel to the goal lines.

iii   *For an offense in In-goal,* penalty kick is to be awarded *only* for offenses under Law 14, Penalty (d) and Law 26 (3) (h).

For an offense under Law 26 (3) (h), the penalty kick is to be taken at whichever is the place where play would restart, that is

- at the twenty-two meter line (at any point the nonoffending team may select), or

- at the center of the half-way line, or

- if a scrummage five meters from the goal line would otherwise have been awarded, at that place or fifteen meters from the touch line on a line five meters from and parallel to the goal line, whichever is the greater.

NOTES

iv   All forms of late tackling should be punished severely. Players who willfully resort to this type of foul play must be sent off the field. A penalty try must be awarded if the late tackle prevents a probably try.

v   It is for the referee to decide what constitutes a dangerous tackle, having regard to the circumstances, e.g., the apparent intentions of the tackler, or the nature of the tackle, or the defenseless position of the player being tackled or knocked over, which may be the cause of serious injury. The referee must always treat a "stiff arm tackle" as foul play.

vi   It is for the referee to determine in the circumstances of the particular case whether the following actions constitute dangerous play:

a) If a player charges or knocks down an opponent carrying the ball without any attempt to grasp him (as in a tackle):

b) If a player taps or pulls the foot or feet of another player who is jumping in a line-out: but this is *prima facie* dangerous play.

vii   If a player is obstructed after kicking the ball and the ball strikes a goal post, the optional penalty should be awarded where the ball alights after bouncing off the post.

viii   If a penalty kick has been awarded and, before the kick has been taken, the offending team infringes Law 26 (3) (h), the referee should

a) caution or send off the player guilty of misconduct and

b) in addition advance the mark for the penalty kick ten meters, this to cover both the original infringement and the misconduct.

ix   If a penalty kick is awarded to a team and before the kick is taken, a player of that team infringes Law 26 (3) (h) the referee should

a) caution or send off the player guilty of misconduct and

b) declare the penalty kick void and

c) award a penalty kick against the team last guilty of misconduct.

x   The referee should note that:

a) Repeated infringement is a question of fact and not a question of whether the offender intended to infringe.

b) If the same player has to be penalized repeatedly he should be dealt with under Law 26 (3) (i).

c) Foul or unfair play must not be condoned.

d) Repeated infringements arise mainly in connection with Scrummages, Off-side and Line-outs. If a player has been penalized for infringing one of these Laws several times in the same match, he should be cautioned and, if he repeats the offense, sent off.

e) It is a question for the referee whether or not a series of the same offenses by different players of a team amounts to repeated infringement. If he considers that it does, he should give a general warning to that team and, if the offense is repeated, he must send the offending player off the field.

f) In deciding the number of offenses which should constitute "repeated infringement" the referee should always apply a strict standard in representative and senior matches. On the third occasion a caution must be given.

In the case of junior or minor matches where ignorance of the Laws and lack of skill may account for many infringements, a less strict standard may be applied.

g) The International Board and the Unions will fully support referees in the strict and uniform enforcement of the Law as to repeated infringements.

Player Ordered Off

A player who is ordered off shall take no further part in the match.

When a player is ordered off, the referee shall, as soon as possible after the match, send to the Union or other disciplinary body having jurisdiction over the match a report naming the player and describing the circumstances which necessitated the ordering off. Such report shall be considered by the Union or other disciplinary body having jurisdiction over the match who shall take such action and inflict such punishment as they see fit.

When a player is ordered off the field under Law 26 in a match played in the United States the referee shall send his report to:

a) the local regional union to which the player's club is affiliated, or

b) if his club or team is not affiliated to a local regional union, to the territorial union in whose area the player's club has its home base, or

c) if the player was playing in a representative match, to the local, territorial or national union for which he was playing, or

d) in the case of a visiting side from abroad, to the local union in whose area the game was played and to the national union of the player's club,

note: In all the above cases the referee shall send a copy of his report to his own referees' society. In addition, if he is not a member of a recognized referees' society, he shall send this report to the local regional union in whose area the game was played.

Club secretaries shall report to their local regional or territorial union, without delay, the name and address of any player of their club who has been ordered off the playing enclosure.

In matches coming within the direct jurisdiction of the U.S.A.R.F.U. any player ordered off may not play again on that same day. The referee himself may decide, without consultation, that this constitutes adequate action for the offense committed, in which case he need only notify the disciplinary committee of the name of the offender and the circumstances of the ordering off, and no committee meeting need be convened. In all other cases the committee must consider whether further punishment is appropriate, in accordance with U.S.A.R.F.U. disciplinary procedures.

Law 27. Penalty Kick.

A penalty kick is a kick awarded to the nonoffending team as stated in the Laws. It may be taken by any player of the nonoffending team and by any form of kick provided that the kicker, if holding the ball, must propel it out of his hands or, if the ball is on the ground, he must propel it a visible distance from the mark. He may keep his hand on the ball while kicking it.

(1) The nonoffending team has the option of taking a scrummage at the mark and shall put in the ball.

(2) When a penalty kick is taken the following shall apply:—

a) The kick must be taken without undue delay.

b) The kick must be taken at or behind the mark on a line through the mark and the kicker may place the ball for a place kick. If the place prescribed by the Laws for the award of a penalty kick is within five meters of the opponents' goal line, the mark for the penalty kick or a scrummage taken instead of it shall be five meters from the goal line on a line through that place.

c) The kicker may kick the ball in any direction and he may play the ball again, without any restriction except:—

- if a kick is taken in In-goal, neither he nor his team may next play the ball until it has travelled beyond the goal line,

- if the kicker has indicated to the referee that he intends to attempt a kick at goal or has taken any action indicating such intention, he must not kick the ball in any other way. Any indication of intention is irrevocable.

d) The **kicker's team** except the placer for a place kick must be behind the ball until it has been kicked.

e) The **opposing team** must run without delay (and continue to do so while the kick is being taken and while the ball is being played by the kicker's team) to or behind a line parallel to the goal lines and ten meters from the mark, or to their own goal line if nearer to the mark. They must there remain motionless with their hands by their sides until the kick has been taken.

Retiring players will not be penalized if their failure to retire ten meters is due to the rapidity with which the kick has been taken, but they may not stop retiring and enter the game until an opponent carrying the ball has run five meters.

f) The **opposing team** must not prevent the kick or interfere with the kicker in any way. This applies to actions such as willfully carrying, throwing or kicking the ball away out of reach of the kicker.

Penalty:—

- For an infringement by the **kicker's team**—a scrummage at the mark.

Penalty:

- For an infringement by the **opposing team**—a penalty kick ten meters in front of the mark or five meters from the goal line whichever is the nearer, on a line through the mark. Any player of the nonoffending team may take the kick.

NOTES

i   The kick must be taken with the ball which was in play unless the referee decides that the ball is defective.

ii The note (ix) under Law 13 applies also in the case of a penalty kick.

iii A player taking a penalty kick may not bounce the ball on his knee. The kick must be made with the foot or lower leg. If a player fails to kick the ball, a scrummage should be ordered.

iv In addition to the general provision regarding waste of time, the kicker is bound to kick without delay, under penalty.

The instructions in the second paragraph of note (i) on Law 13 apply also in the case of a penalty kick.

Even without a caution, if the delay is clearly a breach of Law the kick should be disallowed and a scrummage ordered.

v   The referee must always make up time lost by any delay in taking the kick, as provided for in note (ii) under Law 5.

vi If the kicker appears to be about to take a kick at goal, the referee may ask him to state his intention.

vii If the kicker is taking a kick at goal, all players of the opposing team must remain passive from the time the kicker commences his run until the kick has been taken.

viii When a penalty kick is taken in In-goal and the ball does not travel beyond the goal line a penalty try may be awarded if a defending player, by obstruction, unfair play, foul play or misconduct, prevents an opponent from first grounding the ball. If the infringement by the defending player consists only of playing the ball, a scrummage should be awarded, five meters from the goal line.

ix If, from a penalty kick taken In-goal, the ball travels into touch-in-goal or over the dead-ball line, a five meters scrummage should be ordered, the attacking team to put in the ball.

x   If the kicker takes a drop kick and a goal results, the goal stands even though the kicker has not indicated to the referee an intention to kick at goal.

xi If, notwithstanding a prior infringement by the opposing team, a goal is kicked, the goal should be awarded instead of a further penalty kick.

xii The referee should not award a further penalty if he is satisfied that the reason for such further penalty has been deliberately contrived by the kicker's team, but should allow play to continue.

Law 28. Free Kick.

A free kick is a kick awarded for a fair-catch or to the nonoffending team as stated in the Laws.

A goal may not be scored direct from a free kick.

For an infringement it may be taken by any player of the nonoffending team.

It may be taken by any form of kick provided that the kicker, if holding the ball, must propel it out of his hands, or, if the ball is on the ground, he must propel it a visible distance from the mark. He may keep his hand on the ball while kicking it.

(1) The team awarded a free kick has the option of taking a scrummage at the mark and shall put in the ball.

(2) When a kick is taken, it must be taken without undue delay.

(3) The kick must be taken at or behind the mark on a line through the mark and the kicker may place the ball for a place kick.

(4) If the place prescribed by the Laws for the award of a free kick is within five meters of the opponents' goal line, the mark for the free kick, or the scrummage taken instead of it, shall be five meters from the goal line on a line through that place.

(5) The kicker may kick the ball in any direction and he may play the ball again without restriction except that, if the kick is taken in In-goal, neither he nor his team may next play the ball until it has travelled beyond the goal line.

(6) The **kicker's team**, except a placer for a place kick, must be behind the ball until it has been kicked.

(7) The **opposing team** must not willfilly resort to any action which may delay the taking of a free kick. This includes actions such as willfully carrying, throwing, or kicking the ball away out of reach of the kicker.

(8) The **opposing team** must retire without delay to or behind a line parallel to the goal lines and ten meters from the mark or to their own goal line if nearer to the mark. Having so retired, players of the opposing team may charge with a view to preventing the kick, as soon as the kicker begins his run or offers to kick.

Retiring players will not be penalized if their failure to retire ten meters is due to the rapidity with which the kick has been taken, but they may not stop retiring and enter the game until an opponent carrying the ball has run five meters.

(9) If the kicker kicks the ball from a placer's hands without the ball being on the ground the kick is void.

(10) If having charged fairly, players of the opposing team prevent the kick from being taken it is void.

Penalty:—

- For an infringement by the **kicker's team** or for a void kick—a scrummage at the mark and the **opposing team** shall put in the ball.

If the mark is in In-goal, the scrummage shall be awarded five meters from the goal line on a line through the mark.

Penalty:—

- For an infringement by the **opposing team**—a penalty kick at the mark. If the mark is in In-goal a drop out shall be awarded.

Neither the kicker nor the placer shall willfully do anything which may lead the opposing team to charge prematurely. If either does so, the charge shall not be disallowed.

NOTES

i   The kick must be taken with the ball which was in play unless the referee decides that the ball is defective.

ii   A player taking a free kick may not bounce the ball on his knee. The kick must be made with the foot or lower leg. If a player fails to kick the ball, a scrummage should be ordered.

iii   The kicker may not feint to kick and then draw back. Once he makes any movement to kick, the opponents may charge.

iv   In addition to the general provision regarding waste of time, the kicker is bound to kick without delay, under penalty.

v   The referee shall see that the opposing players do not gradually creep up and that they have both feet behind the ten meters line, otherwise he shall award a penalty kick at the place of the mark.

vi   If the kick is taken from behind the goal line, the ball is in play if an opponent legitimately plays it before it crosses the goal line, and a try may be scored.

vii   When a free kick is taken in In-goal and the ball does not travel beyond the goal line, a penalty try may be awarded if a defending player, by obstruction, unfair play, foul play or misconduct, prevents an opponent from first grounding the ball. If the infringement by the defending players consists only of playing the ball, a scrummage shall be awarded five meters from the goal line on a line through the mark.

viii If from a free kick taken in In-goal, the ball travels into touch-in-goal or over the dead-ball line, a five meters scrummage should be ordered, the attacking team to put in the ball.

ix If opponents lawfully charge down a free kick in the field-of-play, play should be allowed to continue.

x If a free kick has been awarded in the field-of-play and the player retires to his In-goal to take the kick and his opponents having lawfully charged prevent the kick from being taken, a scrummage shall be awarded five meters from the goal line on a line through the mark.

xi If a free kick has been awarded in In-goal and the opponents having lawfully charged prevent the kick from being taken, a scrummage shall be awarded five meters from the goal line on a line through the mark.

xii The referee should not substitute a penalty kick for a free kick if he is satisfied that the reason for such a penalty has been deliberately contrived by the kicker's team, but should allow play to continue.

Index